THE
CHOCOLATE
—BOOK—
VALERIE BARRETT

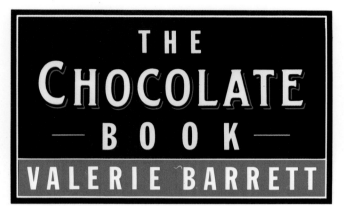

THE CHOCOLATE BOOK

VALERIE BARRETT

CHARTWELL
BOOKS, INC.

A QUINTET BOOK

Published by Chartwell Books Inc.,
A Division of Book Sales Inc.,
110 Enterprise Avenue,
Secaucus, New Jersey 07094

ISBN 0-89009-978-2

This book was designed and produced by
Quintet Publishing Limited
6 Blundell Street, London N7

Art Director Peter Bridgewater
Editor Nicholas Law
Photographer Trevor Wood, Assisted by Michael Bull
Illustrator Lorraine Harrison
Home Economists Felicity Jelliff & Brenda Smith

Typeset in Great Britain by
Central Southern Typesetters, Eastbourne
Colour origination in Hong Kong by
Universal Colour Scanning Limited, Hong Kong
Printed in Hong Kong by Leefung-Asco
Printers Limited

Photograph p.7 courtesy of Rowntree Mackintosh; p.9(top) courtesy of Nestlé Co. Ltd

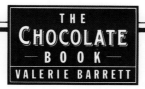

Contents

The History of Chocolate

SMOOTH rich chocolate in its many present day variations has its origins in a simple brown bean. The cocoa bean grows on the cocoa tree and it is believed that the trees originally grew wild in the Amazon. It is probable that when the Mayans migrated to the Yucatan in about AD 600 they established the first cocoa plantations. The Aztecs also used the beans and would have carried them on their travels in Central America.

The beans were used for two purposes. They were used as currency: it is said that 10 beans would buy a rabbit and 100 would buy a slave! The other use to which the cocoa bean was put was as the basis of a bitter foamy drink which had religious and ceremonial significance. This drink, called *chocolatl* (bitter water) was made by mixing roasted ground beans with water or wine which was then beaten until frothy.

Christopher Columbus has been credited with discovering America and as being the first European to see cocoa beans and probably to taste the drink. He returned to the Spanish court with some beans, but they aroused little interest, perhaps because Columbus himself was more interested in his search for new routes to the East. Nothing more happened on the chocolate front for about seventeen years until the Spanish explorer, Cortez, conquered Mexico in 1519. Cortez and his Spanish Conquistadors were invited to the magnificent Aztec court of the Emperor Montezuma. Although Cortez disliked the drink, he was impressed by the way it was served in ornate golden goblets and with the quantity of it drunk by the Emperor and his intimates. He was also quick to recognize the value of the bean as a currency. Cortez therefore established his own cocoa plantation under the Spanish flag. When the Spanish left Mexico, they took some beans with them and planted them in various places as they travelled. Once home, Cortez introduced the chocolate drink to the Spanish court. As the drink was pungent and bitter the Spaniards added sugar and vanilla to it. These additions made the drink much more palatable and it quickly became very popular at court and in high society. Spain began to plant more and more cocoa overseas, but the Spanish kept the secret of its preparation for almost 100 years.

In 1606 an Italian called Antonio Carlotti took the recipe to Italy. From then on the drink spread throughout Europe. When Anne of Austria married Louis XIII of France she brought her own chocolate with her and when the Spanish princess Marie Thérèse married Louis XIV, chocolate was drunk at court, a royal chocolate maker was appointed and chocolate drinking became the rage. Coffee houses, which were already established meeting places in England, were now joined by chocolate houses. These places were the precursors of our present day cafés and bars and they were frequented by politicians, writers and socialites.

The first chocolate factory in America was set up in New England in 1765. Similar factories were also springing up in Europe; Dr Joseph Fry was the first Englishman to manufacture chocolate in a big way. The real breakthrough came in 1828 when a Dutchman called C J Houten patented a process whereby cocoa powder and extract cocoa butter could be obtained from the cocoa mass. Up until this time the whole bean had been ground and used, resulting in a 'fatty' drink. Van Houten's cocoa press squeezed out some of the cocoa butter leaving behind what we now know as cocoa powder. Twenty years later Joseph Fry discovered how to combine the extracted cocoa butter with the chocolate liquor and sugar to make 'eating' chocolate, and in Switzerland, in 1875, Daniel Peter added condensed milk to chocolate and marketed the first solid milk chocolate bar.

A few years later Rodolphe Lindt invented a way of refining chocolate. As long as chocolate was made into a drink it didn't matter if it had lumps and gritty bits as these tended to dissolve or sink with the addition of liquid. However, a solid chocolate bar was a different matter. Lindt's process became known as 'conching' and it consisted of putting the chocolate in heated drums for about 72 hours and rubbing it between rollers or discs. This process gives a silky smoothness to chocolate, allowing it to be poured into different moulds rather than just pressed into 'cakes'.

Since then, the technological changes in the manufacture of chocolate and chocolate products have come fast and furious. From being a luxury that only the rich could afford, chocolate is now an everyday commodity that we take for granted.

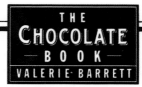

How Chocolate is Grown and Made

THE cocoa bean which gives us both cocoa and chocolate is grown in pods on the *Theobroma cacao*, or cocoa tree. The first cocoa trees probably originated in the Amazon forest more than four thousand years ago. Because the tree is only happy in a tropical climate, it is cultivated only in West Africa, northern and central South America, the Caribbean and some parts of Asia between the tropics of Cancer and Capricorn.

The cocoa tree is extremely sensitive and so the young seeds are grown in special nurseries. After a few months they are transplanted to the cocoa plantation. They need protection from wind and excessive sunlight. This is often provided by banana, coconut or lemon trees, known as 'cocoa mothers', which are planted nearby.

By the time the tree is four or five years old it has dark glossy leaves and ripe fruit in the form of pods growing on both the branches and the trunk. An evergreen, the tree is not dissimilar in size and shape to an English apple tree. The pods are about 7.5–10 cm (3–4 in) wide and 15–25 cm (6–10 in) long and are elongated ovals in shape. They start off a green or red colour and as they ripen the outer shells become hard and turn golden or bright red. Inside the pod are between 20 and 50 plump almond-shaped seeds surrounded by a whitish pulp. These seeds are the precious cocoa beans.

On most plantations there are two harvest seasons, each lasting about three months. The pods have to be cut down from the trees with large steel knives or machetes. They are collected in baskets and taken to be opened. Once split open the beans and pulp are scooped out. At first the beans are creamy beige in colour, but as they are exposed to the air they change to purple. The pulp and the seeds are put into large heaps either on the ground or in boxes or baskets, covered with leaves and left to ferment. The white pulp ferments and produces alcohol and other by-products. The temperature rises and kills off the germ in the cocoa beans so that they cannot sprout, and starts a chain of chemical reactions that remove the bitterness and develop the characteristic chocolate flavour. At the end of fermentation, which can take from two to six days, the beans have turned brown and have become separated from the pulp. They are still wet and have to be spread out in the sun or dried with hot-air blowers to prevent them from rotting. At this stage, checks are made for defects, such as mould or insect damage. The sun gives the beans an even deeper colour and a more aromatic flavour.

How Chocolate is Grown and Made

Sacks of beans are then sent all over the world to various processing plants.

On arrival at the factory, the beans are cleaned and sorted. They are then roasted in a similar way to coffee beans. During roasting the beans become darker brown, the shell becomes brittle and the beans take on their full 'chocolate' aroma. The roasted beans are now put into a machine which cracks them open and an artificial wind or winnower blows away the brittle shell, leaving behind the cocoa 'nibs'.

The nibs are ground between rollers to produce a thick dark paste, or 'chocolate liquor'. This is called the 'mass' and it hardens on cooling. It is sometimes formed into bars at this stage and sold as unsweetened baking chocolate. This 'mass' or chocolate liquor is the basis of all chocolate and cocoa products.

To make cocoa powder, the chocolate liquor is poured into a press. A good percentage of the cocoa butter (a fatty substance found in the bean) is pressed out, leaving a solid, dry cake. This is then crushed, ground and sieved, and the end result is cocoa powder. Cocoa powder is sold just as it is, or it can be mixed with a variety of ingredients such as sugar, starches and milk to produce drinking chocolate or chocolate malted drinks.

Whereas cocoa is made by extracting cocoa butter from the chocolate 'liquor,' chocolate is made by adding extra cocoa butter to it. When sugar is added this produces 'plain' chocolate, and when milk and sugar are added, 'milk' chocolate results. 'White' chocolate is made from cocoa butter only, with the addition of sugar and milk.

When the various ingredients are added to the liquor they are blended in a mixing machine. At this point the mixture is still gritty, so it goes through a series of heavy rollers called a refiner. The chocolate is smooth after this stage, but to make it really silky on the tongue, it has to go through a final treatment known as 'conching.' This stirring process takes place in large drums or conches, from the Spanish *concha*, meaning shell, in which the chocolate is heated and kneaded with rollers. After conching, the liquid chocolate is tempered or cooled so that the fat begins to harden and the chocolate can then be moulded. The filled moulds are cooled, the chocolate removed and wrapped and then sent to the stores. So ends the journey from cocoa bean to chocolate bar.

OPPOSITE ABOVE Theobroma cacao, *the cocoa tree.*
OPPOSITE BELOW *The harvesting of cocoa pods.*
ABOVE *Cocoa beans drying.*
LEFT *The finished product.*

Types of Chocolate

UNSWEETENED CHOCOLATE

(Also known as 'cooking', 'baking' or 'baker's chocolate.') This chocolate is most widely used in the US and Canada and although it is exported it is not always available in Great Britain. The nearest substitute is to use 3 tablespoons cocoa and 1 tablespoon fat to replace 25 g/1 oz unsweetened chocolate. The flavour of unsweetened chocolate is bitter, intense and full-bodied, as it has no sugar or flavourings added.

BITTER CHOCOLATE

Bitter chocolate is available in some delicatessens (Van Houten, Lindt and Suchard are example brands) and it can be used instead of plain chocolate for a strong flavour.

COUVERTURE CHOCOLATE

Couverture chocolate contains a high proportion of cocoa butter which makes it very smooth and glossy. As it has a very brittle texture it needs 'tempering' before use (see page 12). Generally this type of chocolate is only used by professionals. However, it is excellent for coating and moulding and well worth using if you do a lot of chocolate cooking.

MILK CHOCOLATE

Milk chocolate has a much milder flavour than plain as some of the chocolate has been replaced by milk solids. It is best to use this chocolate only in recipes that specifically call for it.

CHOCOLATE CAKE COVERING OR 'COATING' CHOCOLATE

This should not be confused with plain or milk chocolate as it has a certain amount of the cocoa butter replaced by coconut, palm kernel oil or some other vegetable fat. It is much cheaper than plain chocolate and, because it is very easily melted, it is easier to handle. It is good for decorative chocolate recipes, and covering or coating cakes as it does not streak. The only disadvantage is that the flavour is not as strong as plain chocolate.

DIPPING CHOCOLATE

This chocolate makes a good alternative to couverture chocolate. It contains a high proportion of vegetable fat and is good for dipping and moulding.

PLAIN CHOCOLATE

Plain eating chocolate has a good strong flavour and is the most suited for use in cake, dessert and sweet recipes. Plain chocolate is made with chocolate liquor, cocoa butter, vegetable fats, sugar and flavourings.

DRINKING CHOCOLATE

Drinking chocolate is cocoa with a high proportion of sugar. Thus it has a mild, very sweet flavour. Apart from its obvious use in drinks it can be useful as a coating on such things as truffles.

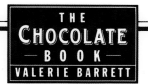

Types of Chocolate

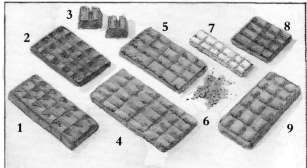

1 Cadbury's Bourneville — Dark Plain.
2 Suchard bittersweet chocolate (Swiss).
3 Bakers chocolate.
4 Lindt milk.
5 Menier cooking milk chocolate.
6 Cocoa.
7 White chocolate.
8 Menier cooking plain.
9 Cadbury's milk.

WHITE CHOCOLATE

This is not really a chocolate at all. It is made from milk, sugar and cocoa butter or another vegetable fat. Generally it is not used for cooking. If you do wish to experiment then take great care when melting it as it can very easily become tight and grainy.

COCOA POWDER

This is chocolate from which the cocoa butter has been removed, before being ground into a powder. Dutch cocoa powder, if available, is darker and slightly less bitter than most as it has been treated with an alkali. Cocoa can be used dry and sieved with other dry ingredients such as flour or icing sugar before being incorporated into a recipe. In some recipes it is better to mix the cocoa to a paste with hot water, thus breaking down the starch cells before cooking.

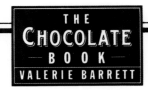
Cooking With Chocolate

OOKING with chocolate as the main ingredient can be quite spectacular, especially when other good quality ingredients are used. To prevent disappointment in your efforts, you must remember to treat chocolate with TLC: tender loving care.

MELTING CHOCOLATE

There are several different ways to melt chocolate, but if you wish to avoid ending up with a solid mass there are a few rules which must be observed. Any equipment used must be perfectly dry because any stray drops of water will cause the chocolate to thicken and stiffen. For the same reason, never cover chocolate when it is being, or has already been melted. If you do end up with a solid mass, try stirring in a little vegetable oil and mix very well. Butter or margarine will not do as they contain some water. The second thing to remember is NEVER to rush the melting process. A watched pot never boils and the temptation is to turn up the heat and speed the process. Unfortunately this will ruin the flavour and texture of the chocolate. It is best to grate or chop the chocolate before melting for a smooth result.

DIRECT HEAT METHOD

This method is only used when the chocolate is combined with butter, sugar or milk, or similar ingredients, as when making some sweets and sauces. The mixture should always be stirred over a very gentle heat. As soon as the mixture has melted it should be removed, to prevent the chocolate over-cooking and becoming 'grainy'.

DOUBLE BOILER METHOD

This is probably one of the best and easiest methods of melting chocolate. If you do not possess a double boiler, one can easily be made by placing a heatproof bowl over a saucepan. The bowl should fit securely on the pan so that neither steam nor water can escape. Water in the saucepan should never touch the bottom of the bowl. Place the chocolate in the bowl. Allow the water in the saucepan to come to the boil and place the bowl on top. Turn off the heat under the saucepan and leave to stand for a while until the chocolate is melted.

OVEN METHOD

Chocolate may be melted in an ovenproof bowl in a very low oven (110°C/225°F/Gas ¼). If the oven has been in use for another purpose and has been turned off, it makes sense to use the lingering heat to melt the chocolate. When the chocolate has almost melted it should be removed and stirred until smooth.

MICROWAVE OVEN METHOD

Microwave ovens are very handy for melting chocolate, especially small quantities, quickly and safely. The chocolate should be broken into small pieces and put into a glass bowl. Microwave, uncovered, until almost melted. The manufacturer's instructions should be followed as the timing and power setting will vary according to the machine.

On average 75 g/3 oz chocolate will melt in 1-1½ minutes. It is important to stir the chocolate just before the end of the cooking time to see if the chocolate has melted and thus prevent overcooking.

HOW TO 'TEMPER' COUVERTURE CHOCOLATE

Generally speaking couverture chocolate is only used by professionals as it is not readily available in shops. However, if you wish to do a lot of chocolate cookery, especially dipping or using moulds, it is worth getting hold of some. Because couverture has a high cocoa butter content it flows and coats excellently. Couverture chocolate must be tempered before using. To do this you will need a thermometer. Break up the chocolate and melt by the double boiler method. Heat the chocolate to a temperature of 38-46°C/100-115°F. Stir well during this heating process. The chocolate then has to be cooled. To do this, remove the bowl to a pan of cold water and cool to 27-28°C/80-82°F, stirring thoroughly. Return the chocolate to the double boiler and re-heat to 31-32°C/88-90°F. Stir all the time and do not exceed this final temperature. The chocolate is now ready to

Cooking With Chocolate

be used. If there is chocolate left over at the end, it can be re-heated without further tempering.

CHOCOLATE FOR DIPPING

Delicious sweetmeats such as marzipan, caramel, fudge, crystallized or fresh fruits can all be dipped in chocolate. Use either tempered couverture, or dipping or plain chocolate. Heat in a double boiler. The ideal temperature for dipping is 36-43°/92-110°F. The temperature should never exceed 49°C/120°F. The chocolate should be in a bowl deep enough for the confection to be totally covered. Using a special dipping fork, fondue fork or thin skewer, lower the confection into the chocolate. Turn it over and then lift out the chocolate, tapping the fork on the edge of the bowl to shake off the excess chocolate. Place the chocolate on a tray lined with non-stick or waxed paper. The dipping fork can be used to decorate the top of the chocolates before they set. Lay the fork on the surface of the chocolate and lift it gently to create raised ridges.

USING MOULDS (MOLDS)

Special moulds can be bought to make eggs, animals (such as rabbits, mice, etc), boxes and so on. They are available in metal or plastic. The plastic ones are cheaper and easier to use in that you can see when the chocolate has shrunk from the sides. The mould must be extremely clean so the chocolate does not stick and has a shiny surface. Wash and rinse the mould and dry very well. Polish well with a soft cloth, kitchen towel or cotton wool.

It is best to use a chocolate that will set hard, so always choose dipping, couverture or plain, good quality, eating chocolate. Melt the chocolate over hot water. The amount will vary according to the size of the mould. Very small moulds will only need one layer, but larger ones will need two, three or four layers. The larger the mould, the thicker the chocolate layer needs to be. Pour the melted chocolate into the mould. Tilt and rotate the mould so that the chocolate evenly coats it. Tip out any excess chocolate. Turn the mould upside down on to a tray lined with non-stick or waxed paper. Put it in a cool place (NOT the refrigerator) until the first layer is just firm to the touch. Repeat as above for subsequent layers. Leave the chocolate to set hard. The chocolate should

have shrunk away from the mould when it is ready.

Very carefully scrape away any chocolate that has gone over the edge of the mould. Gently pull or shake the shape out of the mould. Be careful not to mark the outside with fingerprints! Place the shapes on waxed or non-stick paper. To stick two halves together, as for an Easter egg, brush a little melted chocolate round the rim and press the two halves together. Melted chocolate or royal icing can be used to pipe over any joins on the outside.

STORING CHOCOLATE

Chocolate should be kept in a cool dry place. Contrary to popular belief the refrigerator is not the best place to store chocolate other than for short periods during hot weather. When refrigerated, chocolate will absorb odours very easily and also may collect a film of moisture on the surface. So wrap the chocolate in foil, then in a plastic bag if you wish to refrigerate it. Let the chocolate stand at room temperature before unwrapping and using as this should prevent moisture condensing on the surface.

If chocolate is stored in very warm conditions, the cocoa butter or sugar crystals in it may rise to the surface giving a greyish white 'bloom'. This is completely harmless and although it detracts from the appearance, does not affect the flavour of the chocolate. The 'bloom' will also disappear on melting so the chocolate is quite suitable for cooking.

If you wish to keep chocolate for a longer time in hot conditions, then it is best to freeze it. Again, make sure it is tightly wrapped. Remove it from the freezer the night before you need it, and allow it to thaw completely before unwrapping it. The freezer is an especially good place to store chocolate decorations such as squares, leaves, etc. These can then be used any time to garnish cakes and desserts and only need a few hours to thaw.

If kept in the correct conditions, plain chocolate should keep for one year and milk chocolate for about six months.

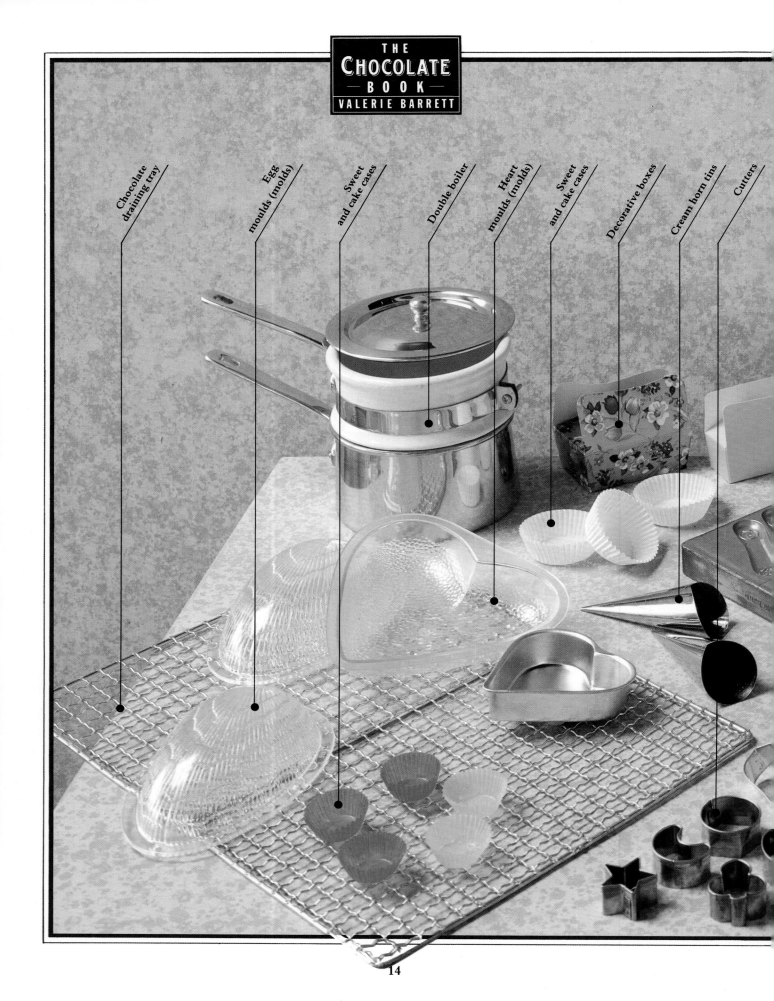

THE
CHOCOLATE
BOOK
VALERIE BARRETT

Chocolate
draining tray

Egg
moulds (molds)

Sweet
and cake cases

Double boiler

Heart
moulds (molds)

Sweet
and cake cases

Decorative boxes

Cream horn tins

Cutters

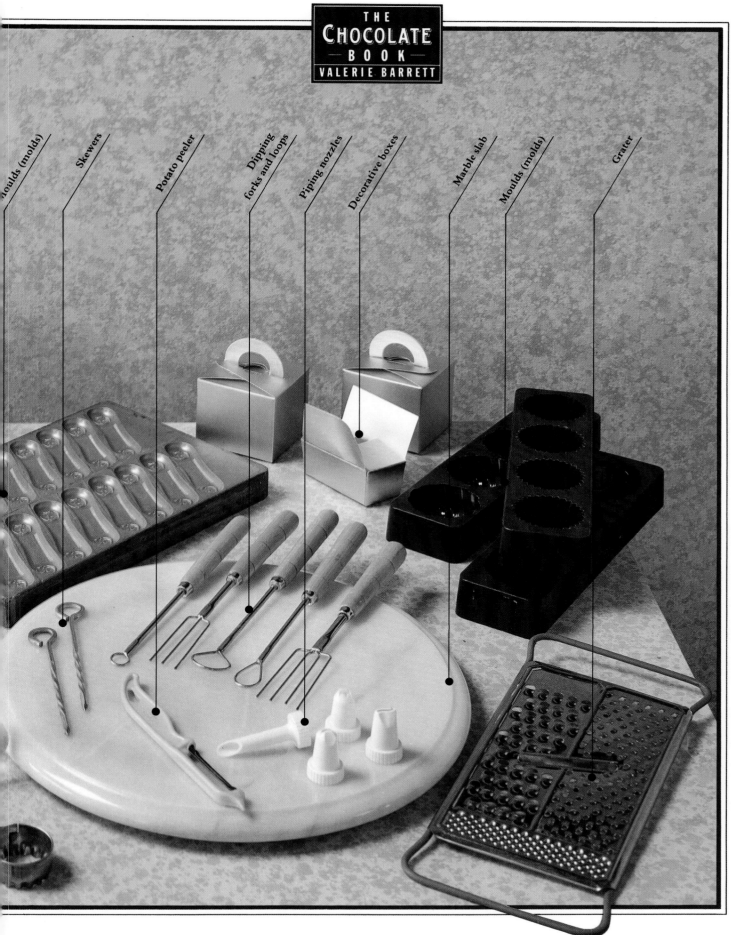

Moulds (molds)

Skewers

Potato peeler

Dipping forks and loops

Piping nozzles

Decorative boxes

Marble slab

Moulds (molds)

Grater

Useful Equipment For Chocolate Cooking

GRATER

For grating chocolate. A stainless steel box or conical-shaped grater with varied cutting edges.

POTATO PEELER

For making chocolate curls. The best type are those with a fixed blade.

SKEWERS OR COCKTAIL STICKS (TOOTHPICKS)

Useful for dipping or the lifting and placing of delicate chocolate decorations.

DIPPING FORKS

These are usually about 20 cm/8 in long, made of stainless steel with wooden handles. They are available in a variety of shapes, from 2, 3 and 4 prongs to round, spiral or triangular shapes. As well as dipping, the forks can be used for marking designs on top of the chocolates.

DOUBLE BOILER

Best made of stainless steel or enamelled steel, this consists of two pans, one made to rest on top and slightly inside the other. Hot water is placed in the bottom pan and the chocolate is melted in the top.

SUGAR BOILING THERMOMETER

Made of brass, the thermometer should be well graduated up to 210°C/400°F. Essential for certain sweetmeat recipes and also for tempering couverture chocolate.

CUTTERS

A selection of various sizes and shapes in steel or plastic. There are very many available now and some make lovely chocolate decorations.

MOULDS

Several different types are available. One type is made of tin, with two halves which clip together when setting. This type makes a solid mould. Other types come in one 'half' of a shape and are used to make hollow moulds. They can be made of stainless steel, semi-rigid plastic or bakelite.

CHOCOLATE DRAINING TRAY

Similar to a cooling rack with a closer tinned wire mesh.

MARBLE SLAB

Not essential, but useful to have for chocolate work as it keeps everything cool.

PIPING BAGS AND NOZZLES

For piping chocolate, medium or small bags are best. In fact, for piping small amounts of chocolate in decorative work it is better to make bags from greaseproof or waxed paper. Star, rope and plain nozzles are the most useful to have.

NON-STICK AND WAXED PAPER

Non-stick (waxed) paper for baking is treated with silicon and is ideal for lining pans or baking trays when working with chocolate. Both types are essential for making chocolate decorations.

SWEET (CANDY) AND CAKE CASES (CUPCAKE PAPERS)

Available in different sizes and qualities. If they are being used for making chocolate cups, choose foil if you can, or else a sturdy paper type.

ICING COMB

Made of plastic or metal, this is useful for making ridged designs on chocolate, such as when making florentines.

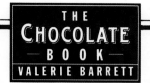

Making Chocolate Decorations

GRATED CHOCOLATE

Chill the chocolate and then rub it across a hand grater. Use either the fine grater or the large grater, depending on the dish you wish to garnish. To prevent clogging, brush the grater every now and then with a dry pastry brush.

CHOCOLATE CURLS

Use chocolate at room temperature (if the chocolate is too cold the curls will break, and if it is too hot they will not curl at all). It is best to use a very thick bar of chocolate. Holding the bar over a plate, draw the blade of a vegetable peeler along the edge and allow the curls to fall on to the plate. Use a toothpick to lift the curls on to the dish to be decorated.

CHOCOLATE SCROLLS

Melt some cooking or plain chocolate and spread out on a cool work surface to a thickness of about 3 mm/⅛ in. Cool until set, but not hard. Using a long firm knife, hold it at an angle of 45° under the chocolate and push away from you, scraping off long curls.

CHOCOLATE CARAQUE

Melt and spread some chocolate as for chocolate scrolls. Using a sharp pointed, long-bladed knife, place it on the surface of the chocolate. Hold the tip of the knife securely in one place. Holding the knife at a slight angle, scrape in a quarter circle movement to produce long, thin slightly cone-shaped curls.

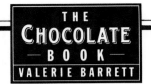

Making Chocolate Decorations

CHOPPED CHOCOLATE

Use chocolate at room temperature. Break into small pieces and place on a chopping board. Using a sharp chopping knife, chop into the size required. Chocolate may also be chopped quite successfully in a food processor.

CHOCOLATE CUPS

Use two thicknesses of paper cake or sweet (candy) cases. If you can obtain foil cases a single layer only is necessary. Melt the chocolate and brush on the bottom and up the sides of the cases. Repeat this process until a thick layer is obtained. Carefully turn upside down onto non-stick (waxed) paper. Chill until hard. Peel paper case away from the chocolate and fill as desired.

CHOCOLATE SQUARES, TRIANGLES,

Melt cooking or plain chocolate and spread evenly onto non-stick (waxed) paper. Leave to set. Using a ruler, mark into squares or rectangles. Cut with a sharp knife. The squares may be cut diagonally to form triangles and the rectangles cut diagonally to form wedges.

CHOCOLATE CUT-OUTS

Melt cooking or plain chocolate and spread evenly on to non-stick (waxed) paper. Leave to set. Using cocktail biscuit or cookie cutters, stamp out shapes, such as hearts, crescents, stars, animals, letters, etc.

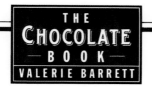

Making Chocolate Decorations

PIPED DESIGNS

Trace the chosen design lightly on a piece of non-stick or waxed paper. Melt the chocolate and pour into a piping bag, fitted with a small plain nozzle. Follow the outline of the design first. Either fill in the centres with solid chocolate or pipe a 'lace' infill. Ideas for piped designs:

Holly leaves: Pipe outlines and then fill in centres.

Simple flower shapes.

Chocolate filigree fans: Outline a fan shape and fill in with 'lace' work.

Butterflies: Cut non-stick paper into small squares. Pipe chocolate on to the paper in a butterfly outline. Fill in the wings with additional lines. Leave until beginning to set. Transfer to an unturned egg carton, placing the butterfly between the cups so it is bent in the centre in the shape of a butterfly. Chill. Carefully remove the paper and position on the chosen dish.

CHOCOLATE HORNS

To make chocolate horns you will need cream horn tins. Make sure the tins are clean and dry, and polish the inside well with kitchen paper (paper towels). Pour a little melted chocolate into the tin, and tilt and turn it until evenly coated. Repeat this process until a thick layer of chocolate is coating the inside of the mould. Leave to set. The chocolate should shrink slightly away from the mould when hard and can be carefully eased out with the point of a knife.

Chocolate-coated ice cream cones can be made in a similar manner. After coating the insides of the ice cream cones with chocolate they can be placed in the freezer for about 10 minutes to harden. They should then be filled with scoops of ice cream and eaten immediately.

CHOCOLATE LEAVES

Select non-toxic fresh leaves with clearly defined veins, such as rose, bay, ivy, strawberry, mint. Wash the leaves and pat dry. Melt some chocolate on a heatproof plate over a pan of hot water. Holding the leaf by the stem carefully dip the veined side only into the chocolate. Or alternatively, brush the chocolate on the leaf with a small paintbrush. Wipe off any chocolate that may have run onto the front of the leaf. Place on non-stick or waxed paper to set. When the chocolate is completely hard, carefully pull off the leaf by the stem.

Biscuits &

Cookies

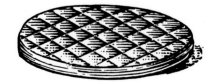

Chocolate Chip Cookies

INGREDIENTS

MAKES ABOUT 30

1 cup + 2 tbsp/125 g/4 oz self-raising flour

¼ cup/25 g/1 oz unsweetened cocoa powder

2.5 ml/½ tsp baking powder

½ cup/125 g/4 oz butter or margarine

⅓ cup/75 g/3 oz brown sugar

¼ cup/50 g/2 oz sugar

2 eggs

2.5 ml/½ tsp vanilla essence (extract)

¾ cup/175 g/6 oz chocolate chips

½ cup/75 g/3 oz chopped walnuts

oven temperature 190°C/375°F/Gas 5

PREPARATION

☛ Sieve together the flour, cocoa and baking powder.

☛ Beat together the butter or margarine and sugars until light and fluffy.

☛ Beat in the eggs one at a time. Add the vanilla.

☛ Add the dry ingredients and beat until well combined.

☛ Stir in the chocolate chips and the nuts.

☛ Drop the dough in heaped teaspoonfuls onto a baking tray. Bake in the oven for about 10 minutes.

☛ Cool for a minute then remove from baking tray and cool on a wire rack.

Chocolate Pinwheels

PREPARATION

☛ Put the butter or margarine and sugar into a bowl and cream together until light and fluffy.

☛ Beat in the egg and vanilla essence.

☛ Work the flour into the creamed mixture.

☛ Divide the mixture in half and knead the cocoa into one half. Shape into two smooth balls. Wrap in cling film (plastic wrap) and chill.

☛ To make pinwheel biscuits (cookies), roll out the plain and chocolate doughs separately into equal rectangles. Brush the plain dough with egg white and place the chocolate mixture on top. Brush the chocolate mixture with egg white.

☛ Roll up like a Swiss roll (jelly roll). Wrap in foil and chill.

☛ Cut into 5-mm/¼-in thick slices. Place on a baking tray and bake for about 8 minutes.

INGREDIENTS

MAKES ABOUT 40

¾ cup/175 g/6 oz butter or margarine

¾ cup/175 g/6 oz sugar

1 large egg, beaten

5 ml/1 tsp vanilla essence (extract)

3¼ cups/350 g/12 oz self-raising flour

45 ml/3 tbsp unsweetened cocoa powder

a little beaten egg white

oven temperature 190°C/375°F/Gas 5

VARIATIONS

☛ To make chequerboard biscuits (cookies) reserve about a quarter of the plain dough.

☛ Shape the remaining plain and chocolate doughs each into two long thin rolls. Brush with egg white.

☛ Put a chocolate roll next to a plain roll. Place the other two rolls on top, reversing the colours. Press lightly together.

☛ Roll out the reserved plain dough to a large rectangle. Brush with egg white and roll it around the four thin rolls. Chill, slice and cook as in recipe above.

☛ To make owl biscuits roll out the plain mixture to a rectangle.

☛ Form the chocolate mixture into a roll. Brush with egg white and roll up in the plain mixture.

☛ Wrap and chill.

☛ Cut into 5-mm/¼-in slices.

☛ To form the owl's head, put two circles side by side. Brush join with egg white and press lightly together.

☛ Pinch the top corners of each head to form ears.

☛ Place almond halves in the centre of each head for the beak. Put two chocolate dots for the eyes.

☛ Cook as in main recipe.

Florentines

INGREDIENTS

MAKES ABOUT 8—10

4 tbsp/50 g/2 oz butter

¼ cup/50 g/2 oz sugar

4 tbsp/25 g/1 oz plain (all-purpose) flour, sieved

⅓ cup/50 g/2 oz almonds, blanched and chopped

½ cup/50 g/2 oz candied peel, chopped

2 tbsp/25 g/1 oz raisins, chopped

1½ tbsp/25 g/1 oz glacé cherries, washed and chopped

rind of ½ lemon, finely grated

125 g/4 oz plain chocolate

oven temperature 180°C/350°F/Gas 4

PREPARATION

☛ Line baking trays with non-stick (waxed) paper.
☛ Put the butter and the sugar into a pan and gently heat them together until melted.
☛ Remove the pan from the heat and stir in the flour.
☛ Add the almonds, peel, raisins, cherries and lemon rind. Stir well.
☛ Put teaspoonfuls of the mixture well apart on the baking trays.
☛ Bake in the oven for about 10 minutes or until golden brown.
☛ While still warm press the edges of the biscuits back to a neat shape. Leave to cool on the baking trays until set. Carefully lift florentines on to a wire rack.
☛ Melt the chocolate. Spread over the smooth sides of the florentines. As the chocolate begins to set, mark into wavy lines with a fork. Leave to set.

Triple Decker Squares

INGREDIENTS

MAKES 16

½ cup/125 g/4 oz butter or margarine

¼ cup/50 g/2 oz sugar

1½ cups/175 g/6 oz plain (all-purpose) flour

FILLING

½ cup/125 g/4 oz butter or margarine

⅓ cup/75 g/3 oz sugar

30 ml/2 tbsp golden syrup (or corn syrup)

¾ cup/196-g/6-oz can condensed milk

TOPPING

175 g/6 oz plain chocolate

30 ml/2 tbsp milk

oven temperature 180°C/350°F/Gas 4

PREPARATION

☛ Cream together the butter or margarine and sugar until light and fluffy.

☛ Stir in the flour. Work the dough with your hands and knead well together.

☛ Roll out and press into a shallow 20-cm/8-in square pan. Prick well with a fork.

☛ Bake in the oven for 25–30 minutes. Cool in the pan.

☛ To make the filling, put all the ingredients into a pan and heat gently, stirring until the sugar has dissolved. Bring to the boil and cook, stirring for 5–7 minutes until golden.

☛ Pour the caramel over the shortbread base and leave to set.

☛ Melt the chocolate and milk together. Spread it evenly over the caramel. Leave until quite cold before cutting into squares.

Viennese Chocolate Biscuits (Cookies)

INGREDIENTS

MAKES ABOUT 20

1 cup/225 g/8 oz butter or margarine

½ cup/50 g/2 oz icing sugar, sieved

2¼ cups/225 g/8 oz plain (all-purpose) flour

½ cup/50 g/2 oz drinking chocolate powder

3 tbsp/25 g/1 oz cornflour (cornstarch)

125 g/4 oz plain chocolate

a little icing sugar

oven temperature 180°C/350°F/Gas 4

PREPARATION

☛ Cream together the butter or margarine and sugar until light and fluffy.

☛ Work in the flour, drinking chocolate powder and cornflour.

☛ Put the mixture into a piping bag fitted with a large star nozzle. Pipe in fingers, or shells, or 's' shapes on to greased baking trays.

☛ Bake in the oven for 20-25 minutes. Cool on a wire rack.

☛ Melt the chocolate. Dip half of each biscuit into the chocolate and leave to set on non-stick (waxed) paper.

☛ Dust the uncoated halves of the biscuits with icing sugar.

VARIATION

☛ To make chocolate gems pipe mixture into small individual star shapes. Bake for about half the time. Place a chocolate button in the centre of each one while still hot.

Small Cakes

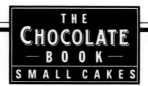
Raspberry Chocolate Eclairs

INGREDIENTS

MAKES ABOUT 10

4 tbsp/50 g/2 oz butter or margarine, cut in pieces

⅔ cup/150 ml/¼ pt water

⅔ cup/65 g/2½ oz plain (all-purpose) flour

2 eggs, beaten

FILLING

⅔ cup/150 ml/¼ pt double (table) cream

1½ cups/225 g/8 oz fresh raspberries

a little sugar

TOPPING

175 g/6 oz plain chocolate

2 tbsp/25 g/1 oz butter

oven temperature 200°C/400°F/Gas 6

PREPARATION

☛ Put the butter or margarine and water into a pan and bring to the boil.

☛ Remove from the heat and tip all the flour into the pan at once. Beat with a wooden spoon until the paste forms a ball. Cool.

☛ Whisk the eggs into the paste, a little at a time. Continue beating until mixture is glossy.

☛ Put pastry into a piping bag fitted with a large plain nozzle. Pipe 7.5-cm/3-in lengths on to greased baking trays.

☛ Bake in the oven for about 25 minutes, until golden brown.

☛ Remove from the oven and make a couple of slits in the sides of each one to allow steam to escape. Return to the oven for a few minutes to dry. Cool on a wire rack.

☛ To make the filling, whisk the cream until stiff. Fold in the raspberries and sugar to taste.

☛ Make a slit down the side of each eclair and fill with the cream mixture.

☛ Melt together the chocolate and butter. Dip the tops of the eclairs into the chocolate and then leave to set.

Chocolate Meringues

INGREDIENTS

MAKES 6–8

3 egg whites

⅓ cup/75 g/3 oz caster sugar

⅔ cup/75 g/3 oz icing sugar, sieved

¼ cup/25 g/1 oz unsweetened cocoa powder, sieved

FILLING

⅔ cup/150 ml/¼ pt double (table) cream

15 ml/1 tbsp soft brown sugar

10 ml/2 tsp unsweetened cocoa powder

oven temperature 110°C/225°F/Gas ¼

PREPARATION

☛ Beat the egg whites until they form stiff peaks. Gradually whisk in the caster sugar, a little at a time.

☛ Whisk in the icing sugar.

☛ Fold in the cocoa powder.

☛ Put the mixture into a piping bag fitted with a large star nozzle. Line baking trays with non-stick (waxed) paper.

☛ Pipe the mixture into spirals.

☛ Bake in the oven for 2–3 hours or until the meringues are dry. Cool on a wire rack.

☛ Whip the cream until stiff. Stir in the sugar and cocoa. Sandwich the meringues together, two at a time, with the chocolate cream.

Butterfly Cakes

INGREDIENTS

MAKES 14–16

½ cup/125 g/4 oz butter or margarine

½ cup/125 g/4 oz sugar

2 eggs

5 ml/1 tsp grated orange rind

½ cup/50 g/2 oz plain chocolate, finely grated

1 cup + 2 tbsp/125 g/4 oz self-raising flour

ICING

6 tbsp/75 g/3 oz butter or margarine

1 cup/175 g/6 oz icing sugar, sieved

75 g/3 oz plain chocolate, melted

DECORATION

icing sugar

seedless raspberry jam or glacé cherries

oven temperature 180°C/350°F/Gas 4

PREPARATION

☛ Put the butter and sugar into a bowl and cream together until light and fluffy.

☛ Beat in the eggs a little at a time. Stir in the orange rind and chocolate.

☛ Fold in the flour.

☛ Arrange paper cases (cupcake papers) in metal bun tin (muffin pan). Divide the mixture between the cases.

☛ Bake in the oven for about 15–20 minutes. Cool.

☛ To make the icing, cream together the butter and icing sugar. Gradually beat in the cooled, melted chocolate.

☛ Starting 5 mm/¼ in in from the edge, remove the top of each cake by cutting in and slightly down to form a cavity.

☛ Pipe a little icing in the cavity of each cake.

☛ Sprinkle the reserved cake tops with icing sugar and cut each one in half. Place each half, cut side outwards, on to the icing to form wings.

☛ Pipe small rosettes of icing in the centre of each cake. Top with a small blob of raspberry jam or half a glacé cherry.

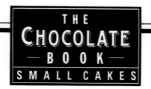
Chocolate Malties

INGREDIENTS

MAKES 20-24

75 g/3 oz plain chocolate

½ cup/75 g/3 oz cream cheese

4 tbsp/50 g/2 oz butter or margarine

1½ tbsp/25 g/1 oz instant malted milk powder

2.5 ml/½ tsp vanilla essence (extract)

2½ cups/375 g/12 oz icing sugar, sieved

45 ml/3 tbsp milk

2 tbsp/200 g/7 oz self-raising flour

2.5 ml/½ tsp baking powder

2 tbsp/25 g/1 oz softened butter or margarine

2 eggs

45 ml/3 tbsp milk

DECORATION

chocolate buttons

oven temperature 180°C/350°F/Gas 4

PREPARATION

☛ Melt the chocolate, cool slightly.

☛ Beat together the cream cheese, butter or margarine, malted milk powder and vanilla essence.

☛ Beat in the icing sugar and milk alternately. Beat in the melted chocolate.

☛ Remove 225 g/8 oz of the chocolate mixture. Cover and reserve for the icing.

☛ Sieve together the flour and baking powder.

☛ Beat the softened butter into the chocolate mixture.

☛ Beat in the eggs.

☛ Stir in the flour alternately with the milk.

☛ Put paper cases (cupcake papers) into patty tins (muffin pans) and fill ⅔ full with the mixture.

☛ Bake in the oven for about 20 minutes. Cool.

TO SERVE

Ice the cakes with the reserved chocolate icing. Decorate with chocolate buttons if you wish.

Chocolate Boxes

INGREDIENTS

MAKES 9

1 egg

1 tbsp/25 g/1 oz sugar

4 tbsp/25 g/1 oz plain (all-purpose) flour

FILLING

⅔ cup/150 ml/¼ pt water

150-g/5-oz pkt (package) tangerine jelly ('jello')

1⅓ cups/225 g/8 oz curd cheese

1¼ cups/300 ml/½ pt double (table) cream

30 ml/2 tbsp apricot jam, sieved

DECORATION

36 × 10 cm (2-in) Chocolate Squares (see page 18)

whipped cream

9 mandarin orange segments

quartered walnuts

oven temperature 200°C/400°F/Gas 6

PREPARATION

☛ Whisk the egg and sugar together until the mixture is thick and creamy and the whisk leaves a trail when lifted.

☛ Using a metal spoon, gently fold in the flour. Pour into a shallow greased and base-lined, 18-cm/7-in square pan.

☛ Bake for 10-12 minutes. Turn out and cool.

☛ Heat the water. Add the jelly and stir until dissolved. Chill until the mixture begins to turn syrupy.

☛ Beat the cheese and gradually add the jelly.

☛ Whip the cream until thick and fold into the cheese mixture. Pour into an 18-cm/7-in square cake pan, lined with non-stick or waxed paper. Chill until set.

☛ Spread the sponge with apricot jam. Unmould the cheese mixture onto the sponge. Trim edges.

☛ Cut the cake into nine squares. Press a chocolate square onto each side of each cake.

TO SERVE

Pipe whipped cream on top of each chocolate box. Top with mandarins and walnuts.

VARIATIONS

☛ Use cherry jelly, cherry jam and top with canned or fresh cherries.

☛ Use strawberry/raspberry jelly, strawberry/raspberry jam and top with fresh strawberries/raspberries.

☛ Use lemon jelly, lemon curd and top with pieces of canned or fresh pineapple.

☛ Use lime jelly, lime marmalade and top with halved slices of kiwi fruit.

Jaffa Cakes

INGREDIENTS

MAKES 18

2 eggs

¼ cup/50 g/2 oz sugar

⅔ cup/65 g/2½ oz self-raising flour, sieved

approx 60 ml/4 tbsp marmalade, sieved

125 g/4 oz plain chocolate

rind of ¼ orange, finely grated

10 ml/2 tsp corn oil

15 ml/1 tbsp water

oven temperature 200°C/400°F/Gas 6

PREPARATION

☞ Put eggs and sugar into a bowl. Whisk until thick and creamy so that when the whisk is lifted the mixture leaves a trail. If using a hand whisk put the bowl over a pan of hot water.

☞ With a metal spoon, fold in the flour.

☞ Spoon the mixture into about 18 well-greased, round-bottomed patty tins (muffin pans). Bake for about 10 minutes until golden brown.

☞ Remove and cool on a wire rack.

☞ Spread a little marmalade over each cake.

☞ Put the chocolate, orange rind, oil and water into a bowl over a pan of hot water. Stir well until melted. Cool until the chocolate starts to thicken and then spoon over the marmalade. Leave to set.

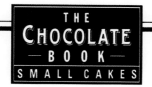
Brownies

INGREDIENTS

MAKES ABOUT 20

1 cup/225 g/8 oz soft brown sugar

½ cup/50 g/2 oz unsweetened cocoa powder, sieved

¾ cup/75 g/3 oz self-raising flour

2 eggs

30 ml/2 tbsp milk

½ cup/125 g/4 oz butter, melted

⅓ cup/50 g/2 oz walnuts, finely chopped

⅓ cup/50 g/2 oz raisins, chopped

ICING

125 g/4 oz plain chocolate

15 ml/1 tbsp black coffee

DECORATION

walnut halves

oven temperature 180°C/350°F/Gas 4

PREPARATION

☛ Mix together the sugar, cocoa and flour.

☛ Beat together the eggs and milk. Stir into the flour mixture, together with the butter, walnuts and raisins.

☛ Spread in a greased and base-lined pan 18 × 28 × 4 cm/7 × 11 × 1½ in.

☛ Bake in the oven for about 30 minutes. Cool.

☛ Melt the chocolate and coffee together. Spread over the cake.

TO SERVE

Decorate with walnut halves. Cut into squares when cold.

Large Cakes

& Gateaux

Chocolate & Sour Cream Marble Cake

INGREDIENTS

175 g/6 oz plain chocolate
1 cup/225 g/8 oz butter
1 cup/225 g/8 oz sugar
4 eggs
3½ cups/350 g/12 oz self-raising flour
⅔ cup/150 ml/¼ pt sour cream
10 ml/2 tsp vanilla essence (extract)
2.5 ml/½ tsp almond essence (extract)
icing sugar

oven temperature 180°C/350°F/Gas 4

PREPARATION

☞ Melt the chocolate and allow to cool slightly.
☞ Cream together the butter and sugar until light and fluffy.
☞ Beat in the eggs one at a time. Add the vanilla and almond essence.
☞ Fold in the flour.
☞ Divide the mixture into two. Add the sour cream to one half and the melted chocolate to the other half.
☞ In a buttered and thickly-sugared 9–10-in/2.6-l/4½-pt Kugelhopf or ring pan, put alternate spoonfuls of the mixtures.
☞ Using a teaspoon, cut down into the mixture and swirl together.
☞ Bake in the oven for about 1 hour.

TO SERVE

Dredge with icing sugar.

Family Chocolate Cake

INGREDIENTS

75 g/3 oz plain chocolate
approx ¼ cup/50 g/2 oz clear honey
½ cup/125 g/4 oz butter or margarine
⅓ cup/75 g/3 oz sugar
2 eggs
1¼ cups/150 g/5 oz self-raising flour
¼ cup/25 g/1 oz unsweetened cocoa powder
7.5 ml/1½ level tsp baking powder
1.25 ml/¼ tsp vanilla essence (extract)
⅔ cup/scant 150 ml/¼ pt milk

ICING

50 g/2 oz plain chocolate
45 ml/3 tbsp water
2 tbsp/25 g/1 oz butter
1⅓ cups/200 g/7 oz icing sugar, sieved

oven temperature 180°C/350°F/Gas 4

PREPARATION

☛ Put the chocolate and honey into a small bowl over a pan of hot water. Stir until the chocolate has melted. Cool.

☛ Cream together the butter or margarine and sugar until light and fluffy.

☛ Beat in the chocolate mixture, then the eggs.

☛ Sieve together the flour, cocoa powder and baking powder.

☛ Stir in the flour mixture a little at a time, alternately with the vanilla essence and milk.

☛ Pour mixture into a lined 19-cm/7½-in round cake pan.

☛ Bake in the oven for about 45 minutes.

☛ Turn on to a wire rack, leaving the lining paper on the cake to form a collar.

☛ When the cake is cool, make the icing. Put the chocolate and water into a small saucepan and melt over a gentle heat.

☛ Remove from the heat and stir in the butter. When the butter has melted, beat in the icing sugar.

☛ Spread the icing over the top of the cake and swirl with a palette knife (metal spatula). When icing is firm, remove the lining paper from the cake.

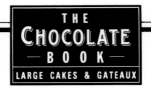

Refrigerator Biscuit Cake

INGREDIENTS

225 g/8 oz milk chocolate

½ cup/125 g/4 oz butter

scant ¼ cup/50 g/2 oz golden syrup (or corn syrup)

⅓ cup/50 g/2 oz raisins, soaked overnight in a little rum

½ cup/50 g/2 oz Brazil nuts, roughly chopped

¼ cup/50 g/2 oz glacé cherries, roughly chopped

*2 cups/225 g/8 oz digestive biscuits
(Graham wafers), crushed*

DECORATION

glacé cherries

whole Brazil nuts

PREPARATION

☛ Put chocolate, butter and golden syrup into a bowl over a pan of hot water.

☛ When the chocolate has melted, stir in the raisins, nuts and cherries.

☛ Add the biscuits and mix well together.

☛ Line a 450-g/1-lb loaf pan. Press the mixture into the pan.

☛ Chill for at least 4 hours, preferably overnight.

☛ Turn out and decorate with glacé cherries and Brazil nuts.

Chequerboard Cake

INGREDIENTS

¾ cup/175 g/6 oz butter or margarine

¾ cup/175 g/6 oz sugar

3 eggs, beaten

1½ cups/175 g/6 oz self-raising flour

15 ml/1 tbsp milk

¼ cup/25 g/1 oz unsweetened cocoa powder

15 ml/1 tbsp boiling water

ginger marmalade

approx 1½ cups/350 g/12 oz marzipan

175 g/6 oz plain chocolate

1 tbsp/15 g/½ oz butter

DECORATION

crystallized ginger

oven temperature 190°C/375°C/Gas 5

PREPARATION

☛ Divide a 20-cm/8-in square cake pan in half by base-lining with foil with a pleat, supported by cardboard, down the centre. Grease well.

☛ Cream together the butter or margarine and sugar. Gradually beat in the eggs.

☛ Fold in the flour. Divide the mixture in half.

☛ Blend the cocoa powder and boiling water together. Stir the milk into one portion and the chocolate paste into the other.

☛ Spoon one flavour into each side of the pan. Bake for about 30 minutes. Turn out. Cool.

☛ Trim each piece of cake and divide in half lengthwise. Sandwich alternately together with marmalade and place one pair of cakes on top of the other to form an oblong with square ends.

☛ Cut a sheet of non-stick or waxed paper big enough to wrap around the cake. Roll the marzipan on top to fit it. Brush the cake with jam. Wrap the marzipan around the cake.

☛ Melt the chocolate with the butter. Spread over the surface of the cake. Decorate with crystallized ginger and leave until set.

Chocolate Meringue Gateau

INGREDIENTS

SERVES 6

3 egg whites

a pinch of cream of tartar

⅔ cup/150 g/5 oz caster sugar

½ cup/75 g/3 oz ground hazelnuts

SPONGE

½ cup/50 g/2 oz plain (all-purpose) flour

½ cup/50 g/2 oz unsweetened cocoa powder

4 eggs, separated

½ cup/125 g/4 oz sugar

FILLING

225 g/8 oz plain chocolate

2 egg yolks

30 ml/2 tbsp water

1¼ cups/300 ml/½pt double (table) cream

¼ cup/50 g/2 oz sugar

red jam

DECORATION

mixed chopped nuts

chocolate curls

icing sugar

oven temperatures 150°C/300°F/Gas 2 (meringues)
and 180°C/350°F/Gas 4 (cake)

PREPARATION

☛ Line two baking trays with non-stick (waxed) paper. Draw an 18-cm/7-in circle on each one.

☛ Put the egg whites and cream of tartar into a bowl and whisk until stiff.

☛ Whisk in the sugar a little at a time until mixture is thick and glossy. Fold in the nuts.

☛ Spread or pipe the meringue in the circles marked on the paper. Bake in the oven for 1 hour. Turn off heat and leave to dry in closed oven for a further ½ hour, or until crisp.

☛ Remove and cool. Carefully peel away the paper.

☛ To make the cake, sieve together the flour and cocoa.

☛ Whisk together the egg yolks and sugar until the mixture is thick and pale.

☛ Whisk the egg whites until thick, but not stiff.

☛ Fold the flour and egg whites alternately into the egg yolk mixture.

☛ Pour into a greased and lined 18-cm/7-in cake pan. Bake for about 40 minutes. Remove and cool.

☛ To make the chocolate cream, melt the chocolate. Cool slightly. Beat together the eggs and water.

☛ Stir the melted chocolate into the egg yolks, mixing well. Put in a pan and cook very gently for a minute. Cool.

☛ Beat together the cream and sugar until soft peaks form. Fold into the chocolate mixture. Cover and chill.

☛ To assemble the gateau, cut the cake into two layers and spread each with a little red jam.

☛ Put a meringue round on a plate and spread with a little chocolate cream. Top with a layer of sponge, spread with cream and place on the second meringue round. Spread with cream and place on the second layer of sponge.

☛ Spread remaining chocolate cream over top and sides of cake.

TO DECORATE

Put chopped nuts round side of cake. Top with chocolate curls and sprinkle with icing sugar.

Mushroom Cake

INGREDIENTS

¼ cup/25 g/1 oz unsweetened cocoa powder

15 ml/1 tbsp boiling water

½ cup/125 g/4 oz butter or margarine

½ cup/125 g/4 oz light, soft brown sugar

2 eggs, beaten

1 cup + 2 tbsp/125 g/4 oz self-raising flour

ICING

½ cup/125 g/4 oz butter or margarine

1⅔ cups/225 g/8 oz icing sugar

50 g/2 oz plain chocolate, melted

approx 1 cup/225 g/8 oz marzipan (preferably 'white')

apricot jam, sieved

icing sugar or drinking chocolate

oven temperature 180°C/350°F/Gas 4

PREPARATION

☛ Mix together the cocoa powder and water to form a paste.

☛ Put butter, sugar and chocolate paste into a bowl and beat until light and fluffy.

☛ Beat in the eggs a little at a time.

☛ Fold in the flour.

☛ Spread the mixture into one greased and base-lined, 20-cm/8-in sandwich cake pan. Bake in the oven for about 25 minutes. Turn out and cool.

☛ To make the icing, cream together the butter or margarine and icing sugar. Stir in the melted chocolate and beat well. Cool.

☛ Using a piping bag fitted with a star nozzle, pipe lines of icing from the edge of the cake to the centre, to represent the underside of a mushroom.

☛ Reserve a small piece of marzipan for the stalk. Roll the remaining marzipan out to a strip about 60 cm/24 in long and wide enough to stand just above the sides of the cake.

☛ Brush the sides of the cake with apricot jam. Press the marzipan strip round the edge of the cake. Curve the top of the marzipan over the piped ridges.

☛ Shape the reserved marzipan into a stalk and place in centre of cake. Sieve a little icing sugar or drinking chocolate over the icing on the cake.

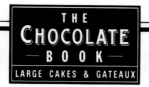
Surprise Chocolate Ring

INGREDIENTS

SERVES 8

1¼ cups/150 g/5 oz self-raising flour

¼ cup/25 g/1 oz unsweetened cocoa powder

¾ cup/175 g/6 oz soft margarine

¾ cup/175 g/6 oz sugar

3 eggs

60 ml/4 tbsp cherry brandy

1 cup/125 g/4 oz fruit (eg strawberries, raspberries, stoned cherries)

⅔ cup/150 ml/¼ pt double (table) cream

ICING

generous ¼ cup/65 ml/2½ fl oz double (table) cream

1½ cups/175 g/6 oz plain chocolate, grated

DECORATION

Piped Chocolate Butterflies (see page 19) or Chocolate Dipped Fruits (see page 110)

oven temperature 180°C/350°F/Gas 4

PREPARATION

☛ Sieve the flour and cocoa into a mixing bowl. Add the margarine, sugar and eggs. Beat well together.

☛ Spoon mixture into a greased and floured 8-in/1.2-l/2-pt ring mould (mold). Bake in the oven for about 35-40 minutes. Turn out and cool.

☛ Turn the cake upside down and cut a slice about 2 cm/¾ in deep off the flat base of the ring. Lift off the slice carefully and reserve.

☛ With a teaspoon, scoop out the cake in a channel about 2 cm/¾ in deep and 2.5 cm/1 in wide.

☛ Sprinkle 45 ml/3 tbsp of the cherry brandy over the sponge.

☛ Chop the fruit and spread in the hollow.

☛ Whisk the cream until stiff. Stir in remaining brandy. Spread the cream over the fruit.

☛ Place the reserved slice back on the cake.

☛ Invert the cake so it is the right way up.

☛ To make the icing, put the cream into a saucepan and bring just to the boil. Add the chocolate. Stir until the chocolate melts.

☛ Cool until the mixture is thick and smooth. Pour over the cake.

☛ Put in a cool place until set.

TO SERVE

Decorate with piped chocolate butterflies or chocolate dipped fruit.

Black Forest Cake

INGREDIENTS

8 eggs, separated

1 cup/225 g/8 oz sugar

1½ cups/75 g/3 oz cake crumbs (e.g. Madeira cake)

⅔ cup/75 g/3 oz ground almonds

½ cup/50 g/2 oz plain (all-purpose) flour

½ cup/50 g/2 oz unsweetened cocoa powder

FILLING

approx 2½ cups/450 g/1 lb stoned and cooked or canned black cherries

¼ cup + 2 tsp/75 ml/2½ fl oz cherry juice

½ cup/120 ml/4 fl oz kirsch

2½ cups/600 ml/1 pt double (table) cream, whipped

grated chocolate

redcurrant jelly, warmed

Chocolate Caraque or Curls (see page 17)

icing sugar

oven temperature 180°C/350°F/Gas 4

PREPARATION

☛ Grease and line two 23-cm/9-in sponge cake pans
☛ Beat the egg yolks and sugar together until thick and the mixture leaves a trail.
☛ Fold in the cake crumbs and almonds.
☛ Sieve together the flour and cocoa. Whisk the egg whites until stiff.
☛ Fold in the flour and egg whites into the cake mixture. Turn into the prepared pans. Bake in the oven for about 35 minutes until springy to the touch. Turn out and cool on a wire rack.
☛ Reserve some of the cherries for decoration.
☛ Split each sponge into two, to give 4 layers.
☛ Mix together the juice and kirsch. Sprinkle a little over a sponge. Spread with a little cream and top with a few cherries.
☛ Lay a second sponge on top and repeat the layering process. Repeat with the third sponge layer.
☛ Top with the last sponge layer and spread the surface and sides with the remaining whipped cream.
☛ Press grated chocolate firmly over the sides with a palette knife (metal spatula).
☛ Pipe two rows of cream around the top edge of the cake, leaving a space between the width of a cherry. Place the reserved cherries between the rows of cream. Brush the cherries lightly with a little warmed redcurrant jelly.

TO SERVE

Pile Chocolate Caraque or Curls in the centre of the cake. Sprinkle lightly with icing sugar.

Sachertorte

INGREDIENTS

225 g/8 oz plain chocolate

½ cup/125 g/4 oz unsalted butter

¾ cup/175 g/6 oz sugar

5 eggs, separated

⅔ cup/75 g/3 oz ground hazelnuts or almonds

½ cup/50 g/2 oz self-raising flour, sieved

FILLING

⅔ cup/150 ml/¼ pt double (table) cream, whipped

ICING

225 g/8 oz plain chocolate

½ cup/125 g/4 oz butter, melted

DECORATION

whipped cream

whole hazelnuts

Chocolate Leaves (see page 19)

oven temperature 180°C/350°F/Gas 4

PREPARATION

☛ Melt the chocolate in a bowl over a saucepan of hot water. Add the butter, cut into small pieces, and beat until the butter has melted and the mixture is smooth.

☛ Beat in the caster sugar. Gradually add the egg yolks, beating well between each addition.

☛ Whisk the egg whites until stiff. Gently fold into the chocolate, together with the ground nuts and flour.

☛ Put the mixture into two greased and base-lined 20-cm/8-in sandwich cake pans. Bake for 20-25 minutes. Cool on a wire rack.

☛ When the cakes are cold, sandwich together with whipped cream.

☛ To make the icing, melt the chocolate and gradually add the butter, beating well between each addition. Leave for 20-30 minutes, until cold, and of a coating consistency.

☛ Spread the icing over the top and sides of the cake. Leave until set.

☛ Decorate with piped whipped cream, hazelnuts and Chocolate Leaves.

Dobos Torte

INGREDIENTS

6 eggs, separated

rind of 1 lemon, grated

¾ cup/175 g/6 oz sugar

1½ cups/150 g/5 oz plain (all-purpose) flour, sieved

BUTTER CREAM

225 g/8 oz plain chocolate

1 cup/225 g/8 oz butter

3½ cups/450 g/1 lb icing sugar, sieved

CARAMEL

¾ cup/175 g/6 oz granulated sugar

oven temperature 200°C/400°F/Gas 6

PREPARATION

☛ Grease and flour 7 flat surfaces, such as baking trays and roasting pans. Using a cake pan or plate, mark a circle 20-cm/8-in diameter on each one.
☛ Whisk the yolks with the lemon rind and sugar in a mixing bowl until the mixture is thick.

☛ Whisk the egg whites until stiff.
☛ Fold the egg whites and flour alternately into the egg yolk mixture.
☛ Divide the mixture evenly between the circles. Bake in batches in the oven for about 8 minutes, or until golden brown. Lift onto wire racks to cool.
☛ Use the 20-cm/8-in cake pan or plate to trim edges so that all the circles are the same size.
☛ To make the butter cream, melt the chocolate. Add the butter and stir until melted. Cool. Beat in the sieved icing sugar.
☛ To make the caramel, put the sugar into a heavy saucepan. Heat very slowly over a low heat, stirring until the sugar is completely dissolved. Heat until the caramel turns golden brown.
☛ Pour the caramel immediately on to one of the cake layers. Before the caramel sets, cut the cake layer into 8 sections, using an oiled or buttered knife.
☛ Sandwich the remaining cake layers together with some of the chocolate butter cream. Spread butter cream round the sides of the cake.
☛ Put the remaining butter cream into a piping bag, fitted with a star nozzle. Pipe eight long whirls on top of the cake, radiating out from the centre. Set a caramel-coated section, tilted slightly, on each whirl.

Torta Sorentina (Easter Cake)

INGREDIENTS

1 cup/225 g/8 oz unsalted butter
4 large eggs
1 cup/225 g/8 oz sugar
2¼ cups/225 g/8 oz self-raising flour
rind of ½ lemon, grated

LEMON FILLING

1 egg white
½ cup/50 g/2 oz icing sugar
6 tbsp/75 g/3 oz unsalted butter
rind of ½ lemon, grated

ICING

175 g/6 oz plain chocolate
30 ml/2 tbsp cream
2 tbsp/25 g/1 oz butter

DECORATION

crystallized lemon slices

oven temperature 180°C/350°F/Gas 4

PREPARATION

☛ Melt the butter and leave to cool.

☛ Put eggs and sugar into a bowl over a pan of hot water and whisk until they are pale and thick and leave a trail.

☛ Gently fold in the flour, rind and butter. Do not overmix.

☛ Pour into a greased and floured 2-l/3½-pt ring pan. Bake in the oven for 30-40 minutes. Cool slightly, then turn out on to a wire rack.

☛ To make the filling, put the egg white and icing sugar into a bowl over a pan of hot water and whisk until a meringue is formed. Remove from heat and whisk until cool.

☛ Beat the butter until light and fluffy. Beat in the meringue a little at a time. Add the lemon rind.

☛ Split the cake into three layers. Spread the lemon filling between the layers. Chill.

☛ Put the chocolate and cream in a bowl over a pan of hot water. When melted, stir in the butter. Remove from heat and mix until smooth.

☛ Coat the cake with the icing. Decorate with crystallized lemon slices. Allow icing to set.

Buche De Noël

INGREDIENTS

4 eggs, separated
½ cup/125 g/4 oz sugar
1 cup + 2 tbsp/125 g/4 oz plain (all-purpose) flour
BUTTER CREAM
⅓ cup/75 g/3 oz sugar
6 tbsp/85 ml/3 fl oz water
4 egg yolks
¾ cup/175 g/6 oz unsalted butter
75 g/3 oz plain chocolate, melted
5-10 ml/1-2 tsp dark rum
DECORATION
Meringue Mushrooms (see page 112)
marzipan, holly leaves and berries

oven temperature 230°C/450°F/Gas 8

PREPARATION

☛ Grease and line a 23 × 33-cm/9 × 13-in Swiss roll (jelly roll) pan.

☛ Put egg yolks and sugar into a mixing bowl and whisk until the mixture falls in a thick trail.

☛ Whisk the egg whites until stiff.

☛ Fold the egg whites and flour alternately into the egg yolk mixture. Pour into the pan and bake in the oven for about 10 minutes until golden brown.

☛ Put a sheet of greaseproof or waxed paper on top of a dampened tea towel and sprinkle with caster sugar. Turn sponge out on to the sugared paper.

☛ Peel off the lining paper and quickly trim the edges of the sponge. Make a shallow groove across one short side of the cake 2.5 cm/1 in from the edge.

☛ Fold the sponge over at the groove. Using the towel to support the cake, roll up the sponge with the greaseproof paper inside. Cover with the damp cloth until cold.

☛ To make the butter cream, put the sugar and water into a small pan. Dissolve the sugar and then bring to the boil and boil to the 'thread' stage (110°C/225°F).

☛ Whisk the egg yolks in a bowl until thick and creamy. Slowly pour the hot syrup on the egg yolks in a steady stream, beating constantly until the mixture is light and fluffy.

☛ Beat the butter until soft. Add the egg mixture a little at a time until the mixture is firm and shiny. Stir in the chocolate and rum.

☛ Carefully unroll the sponge and remove the greaseproof paper. Spread a little butter cream over the sponge and roll up again.

☛ Put the cake on to a serving dish. Spoon the remaining butter cream into a piping bag fitted with a star nozzle. Pipe lines lengthways down the cake. Add an occasional swirl to represent a 'knot' on a log.

TO SERVE

Decorate with Meringue Mushrooms and marzipan, holly leaves and berries.

Pies

Chocolate Chiffon Pie

INGREDIENTS

SERVES 6

*175 g/6 oz shortcrust pastry
(recipe for 1 pie shell)*

⅔ cup/150 ml/¼ pt milk

⅓ cup/75 g/3 oz sugar

½ cup/125 g/4 oz plain chocolate, chopped

2 small eggs, separated

10ml/2 tsp powdered gelatine (gelatin)

30 ml/2 tbsp water

⅔ cup/150 ml/¼ pt double (table) cream

DECORATION

whipped cream

chocolate curls

oven temperature 190°C/375°F/Gas 5

PREPARATION

☛ Roll out the pastry and use to line a 20-cm/8-in flan tin (pie plate). Bake 'blind' (lined with grease-proof [waxed] paper and baking beans) in the oven for 20-25 minutes. Remove greaseproof paper and baking beans and return to oven for a further 5-10 minutes until crisp and lightly browned. Leave to cool.

☛ Put the milk, ⅓ cup/75 g/3 oz sugar and chocolate into a saucepan and melt over a gentle heat. Stir continuously. Cool slightly.

☛ Whisk the egg yolks into the chocolate mixture.

☛ Dissolve the gelatine in the water and stir into chocolate. Leave until the mixture is beginning to thicken and set.

☛ Whisk egg whites until stiff. Whisk in the remaining sugar.

☛ Whisk the cream until it stands in soft peaks.

☛ Fold the egg whites and cream thoroughly into the chocolate mixture. Pour into the pastry case.

☛ Chill until set.

TO SERVE

Pipe whipped cream over the top and pile chocolate curls in the centre.

Chocolate Syrup Tart

INGREDIENTS

SERVES 8

2¼ cups/225 g/8 oz plain (all-purpose) flour

30 ml/2 tbsp icing sugar

1 cup/225 g/8 oz butter

a little water

125 g/4 oz plain chocolate

3 eggs

45 ml/3 tbsp golden syrup (or corn syrup)

1 cup/225 g/8 oz sugar

5 ml/1 tsp vanilla essence (extract)

TO SERVE

vanilla ice cream

oven temperature 180°C/350°F/Gas 4

PREPARATION

☛ Sieve the flour and icing sugar into a bowl. Rub in ½ cup/150 g/5 oz butter until the mixture resembles fine crumbs.

☛ Add enough water to mix to a stiff dough.

☛ Roll out pastry and use to line a 23-cm/9-in pie plate.

☛ Put the remaining butter and the chocolate into a saucepan. Stir over gentle heat until melted and blended.

☛ Beat the eggs, syrup, sugar and essence together. Stir in the chocolate mixture.

☛ Pour filling into the pastry case. Bake in the oven for about 40 minutes, until the top is crunchy and the filling set. (The filling should be soft inside.)

TO SERVE

Serve warm with scoops of vanilla ice cream.

Rich Chocolate Meringue Pie

INGREDIENTS

SERVES 6

2 cups/225 g/8 oz digestive biscuits (Graham wafers)

½ cup/125 g/4 oz butter

FILLING

1 tbsp/25 g/1 oz sugar

4 tbsp/25 g/1 oz plain (all-purpose) flour

10 ml/2 level tsp cornflour (cornstarch)

2 large eggs, separated

1¼ cups/300 ml/½ pt milk

2 tbsp/25 g/1 oz butter

1 cup/125 g/4 oz plain chocolate, finely chopped

10 ml/2 tsp rum (optional)

TOPPING

½ cup/4 oz caster sugar

ground cinnamon

oven temperature 200°C/400°F/Gas 6

PREPARATION

☛ Crush the biscuits or wafers until they resemble fine breadcrumbs.

☛ Melt the butter and stir into the biscuits. Press the biscuits over the base and sides of a 20-cm/8-in ovenproof flan dish (pie plate).

☛ Blend together the sugar, flour, cornflour, egg yolks and a little of the milk. Heat the remaining milk.

☛ Stir the hot milk on to the flour mixture and whisk well. Return the mixture to the pan. Heat gently, stirring until the mixture thickens.

☛ Stir in the butter, chocolate and rum if used. Stir until smooth. Pour into the biscuit pie shell. Chill.

☛ About ½ hour before serving, make the meringue topping. Whisk the egg whites until stiff.

☛ Whisk in half the sugar a teaspoonful at a time. Add the remaining sugar and whisk well.

☛ Spread the meringue over the chocolate flan. Swirl decoratively with a teaspoon.

☛ Bake in the oven for 3-5 minutes, until meringue is golden brown.

☛ Sprinkle with a little ground cinnamon.

Mississippi Mud Pie

INGREDIENTS

SERVES 8

1½ cups/175 g/6 oz digestive biscuits (Graham wafers)

large knob butter, melted

125 g/4 oz plain chocolate, melted

5 cups/1.1 l/2 pt coffee ice cream

5 cups/1.1 l/2 pt chocolate ice cream

30 ml/2 tbsp Tia Maria

30 ml/2 tbsp brandy

DECORATION

whipped cream

grated chocolate

PREPARATION

☛ Crush the biscuits or wafers in a food processor or in a polythene bag (plastic bag) with a rolling pin.
☛ Stir in the butter and chocolate and mix well together.
☛ Press the crumbs firmly and evenly over the bottom and sides of a greased 23-cm/9-in flan dish (pie plate). Chill.
☛ Allow the ice creams to soften slightly. Put in a bowl and add the liqueur and brandy. Blend well together.
☛ Spoon the ice cream into the chocolate case and put in the freezer until solid.

TO SERVE

Remove pie from freezer about 15 minutes before serving. Decorate with whipped cream and grated chocolate.

Breads

Chocolate Waffles

INGREDIENTS

1½ cups/150 g/5 oz plain (all-purpose) flour

¼ cup/25 g/1 oz unsweetened cocoa powder

a pinch of salt

10 ml/2 level tsp baking powder (baking soda)

1 tbsp/25 g/1 oz sugar

2 eggs, separated

1¼ cups/300 ml/½ pt milk

4 tbsp/50 g/2 oz butter, melted

TO SERVE

60 ml/4 tbsp Chocolate Syrup (see page 117)

60 ml/4 tbsp maple syrup

¼-⅓ cup/25-50 g/1-2 oz pecan nuts, chopped

PREPARATION

☞ Sieve together the flour, cocoa, salt and baking powder. Stir in the sugar.
☞ Make a well in the centre and add the egg yolks, milk and butter. Stir well together.
☞ Whisk the egg whites until stiff. Fold lightly into the batter.
☞ Pour the batter into a heated waffle iron and cook.

TO SERVE

Mix together the chocolate and maple syrups and stir in the nuts. Serve the waffles immediately with the sauce poured over.

Chocolate Croissants

INGREDIENTS

MAKES ABOUT 12
4½ cups/450 g/1 lb strong white (bread) flour
5 ml/1 tsp salt
2 tbsp/25 g/1 oz lard
1½ tbsp/25 g/1 oz fresh yeast
1 cup/225 ml/8 fl oz tepid water
1 egg, beaten
¾ cup/175 g/6 oz butter
1 cup/225 g/8 oz chocolate chips
1 egg, beaten
10 ml/2 tsp water
5 ml/1 tsp sugar

oven temperature 220°C/425°F/Gas 7

PREPARATION

☛ Sieve together the flour and salt. Rub in the lard.

☛ Blend the yeast with the water. Add the yeast liquid and egg to the flour and mix to a soft dough.

☛ Knead lightly on a floured surface for 10–15 minutes until smooth. Roll out to a strip 51 × 20 cm/ 20 × 8 in.

☛ Soften the butter and divide into 3. Dot one portion of the butter over two-thirds of the dough. Fold the dough in three, folding up the unbuttered portion first. Seal edge with a rolling pin. Wrap in cling film (plastic wrap) and chill.

☛ Repeat twice more, using the other two portions of butter. Wrap in cling film (plastic wrap) and chill.

☛ Roll out and fold three more times. Chill for at least one hour.

☛ Roll out to a rectangle 55 × 30.5 cm/22 × 12 in. Trim the edges and cut in half lengthways. Cut each strip into triangles.

☛ At the base end of each triangle put a little pile of chocolate chips.

☛ Beat together the egg, water and sugar. Brush over the edges of each croissant.

☛ Roll up each croissant loosely starting at the base and finishing with the tip underneath.

☛ Put on to a baking sheet and shape.

☛ Cover with oiled polythene (plastic wrap) and leave to rise for 20–30 minutes. Brush with glaze.

☛ Bake in the oven for about 20 minutes. Cool on a wire rack. Serve warm.

Danish Pastries

INGREDIENTS

MAKES ABOUT 16

1½ tbsp/25 g/1 oz fresh yeast

⅔ cup/150 ml/¼ pint tepid water

4½ cups/450 g/1 lb plain (all-purpose) flour

a pinch of salt

4 tbsp/50 g/2 oz lard

30 ml/2 tbsp sugar

2 eggs, beaten

1¼ cup/275 g/10 oz butter

FILLING

4 tbsp/50 g/2 oz butter

¾ cup/125 g/4 oz icing sugar, sieved

75 g/3 oz plain chocolate, melted

1½ tbsp/25 g/1 oz toasted almonds, finely chopped

a few drops of almond essence

GLAZE

1 egg, beaten

honey

oven temperature 220°C/425°F/Gas 7

PREPARATION

☛ Blend the yeast and water together.

☛ Sieve flour and salt into a bowl and rub in the lard. Stir in the sugar.

☛ Add the yeast liquid and eggs to the flour and mix to a smooth elastic dough. Knead lightly. Put into a lightly-oiled bowl and cover with cling film (plastic wrap). Chill for 10 minutes.

☛ Soften the butter and shape into a flat oblong on greaseproof (waxed) paper.

☛ Roll out the dough on a floured surface to a rectangle three times the size of the butter.

☛ Place the butter in the centre of the dough and fold the dough over to enclose it. Press the rolling pin firmly along the open sides.

☛ Give the dough a quarter turn and roll out to a rectangle three times as long as it is wide.

☛ Fold into three. Wrap in cling film (plastic wrap) and chill for 10 minutes. Repeat the rolling and folding three more times.

☛ To make the filling, beat together the butter and icing sugar. Beat in the chocolate, almonds and essence. Chill.

☛ Roll out the dough thinly and cut into 7.5-cm/ 3-in squares.

☛ Put a rounded teaspoonful of filling on to the centre of each square. Bring two opposite corners of the dough to the centre. Either seal with beaten egg or insert a wooden cocktail stick (toothpick) through.

☛ Place on a greased baking sheet. Cover with greased cling film (plastic wrap) and leave to prove (proof) for about 30 minutes.

☛ Brush with beaten egg. Bake for about 20 minutes.

☛ Brush with a little honey whilst warm.

Chocolate Muffins

INGREDIENTS

MAKES 12

2¼ cups/225 g/8 oz plain (all-purpose) flour

45 ml/3 tbsp unsweetened cocoa powder

¼ cup/50 g/2 oz sugar

15 ml/1 level tbsp baking powder (baking soda)

a pinch of salt

50 g/2 oz raisins

1 egg, beaten

1 cup/225 ml/8 fl oz milk

¼ cup/50 ml/2 fl oz corn oil

oven temperature 200°C/400°F/Gas 6

PREPARATION

☛ Sieve the flour and cocoa into a bowl. Stir in the sugar, baking powder, salt and raisins.
☛ Beat together the egg, milk and oil.
☛ Add the liquid to the dry ingredients all at once, and mix quickly together. Do not over-mix.
☛ Spoon the mixture into 12 greased 6.5-cm/2½-in deep bun or muffin pans.
☛ Bake for about 20 minutes.
☛ Turn out on to a wire rack. Serve them warm, split and buttered.

Chocolate Ring Doughnuts

INGREDIENTS

MAKES ABOUT 12

2¼ cups/225 g/8 oz plain (all-purpose) flour

2.5 ml/½ tsp bicarbonate of soda (baking soda)

5 ml/1 tsp cream of tartar

2 tbsp/25 g/1 oz butter

¼ cup/50 g/2 oz soft brown sugar

50 g/2 oz plain chocolate

5 ml/1 tsp vanilla essence (extract)

1 egg, beaten

milk

oil for deep frying

caster sugar mixed with ground cinnamon

ICING

125 g/4 oz plain chocolate

60 ml/4 tbsp milk and water mixed

1⅔ cups/225 g/8 oz icing sugar, sieved

frying temperature 182°C/360°F

PREPARATION

☛ Sieve the flour, bicarbonate of soda and cream of tartar into a bowl.

☛ Rub in the butter and stir in the sugar.

☛ Melt the vanilla essence and chocolate together.

☛ Pour the beaten egg and chocolate into the dry ingredients and mix to a stiff dough, adding a little milk if necessary.

☛ Knead very lightly and roll out until about 1 cm/½ in thick.

☛ Using a floured ring cutter (or a large and small round pastry cutter). Stamp out doughnuts. Reserve the centres.

☛ Heat the oil and fry the doughnuts a few at a time until golden brown. Drain and cool.

☛ Cook the doughnut centres (called doughnut 'holes'). Drain. While still warm toss in caster sugar which has cinnamon added to it. Serve doughnut 'holes' warm.

☛ To make the icing, melt the chocolate and liquid together. Add the icing sugar and beat well.

☛ Spread icing over cooled doughnut rings.

These are always best eaten on the day they are made.

Chocolate Caramel Pecan Bread

INGREDIENTS

MAKES 9 ROLLS

2¼ cups/225 g/8 oz strong white (bread) flour

1 tbsp/15 g/½ oz fresh yeast

5 ml/1 tsp sugar

½ cup/100 ml/4 fl oz tepid milk

2.5 ml/½ tsp salt

2 tbsp/25 g/1 oz butter

1 egg, beaten

25 g/1 oz butter, melted

50 g/2 oz plain chocolate

¾ cup/75 g/3 oz pecan nuts, chopped

2.5 ml/½ tsp mixed spice

¼ cup/50 g/2 oz soft brown sugar

GLAZE

125 g/4 oz plain chocolate

2 tbsp/25 g/1 oz butter

15 ml/1 tbsp honey

oven temperature 190°C/375°F/Gas 5

PREPARATION

☛ Sieve ½ cup/50 g/2 oz of the flour into a bowl. Add the yeast, sugar and milk and mix to a smooth batter.

☛ Leave in a warm place 10-20 minutes or until frothy.

☛ Sieve remaining flour with the salt into a bowl and rub in the butter. Add to the yeast batter. Stir in the egg and mix to a soft dough.

☛ Knead on a lightly-floured surface for about 5 minutes until smooth. Put into a lightly-oiled bowl. Cover with cling film (plastic wrap) and leave to rise in a warm place for about 1 hour or until double in size.

☛ Knead well. Roll out to an oblong about 30 × 23 cm/12 × 9 in. Melt together the butter and chocolate and brush over the dough.

☛ Mix together the nuts, spice and sugar and sprinkle over the dough.

☛ Roll up lengthways, like a Swiss roll (jelly roll). Cut into nine slices.

☛ Grease an 18-cm/7-in square cake pan. Place the slices, cut side down, in the pan. Cover with oiled cling film and leave to rise in a warm place for about 30 minutes.

☛ Remove cling film and bake in the oven for about 30 minutes.

☛ Turn out onto a wire rack. Melt together the chocolate, butter and honey. Drizzle over the bread whilst warm. Serve warm.

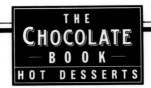
Hot Desserts

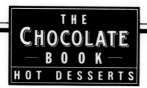
Banana Choc-Chip Pudding

INGREDIENTS

SERVES 4–5

½ cup/125 g/4 oz butter or margarine

½ cup/125 g/4 oz sugar

2 eggs, beaten

¼ cup/150 g/5 oz self-raising flour

¼ cup/25 g/1 oz unsweetened cocoa powder

approximately 30 ml/2 tbsp milk

1 small banana, peeled and chopped

¼ cup/50 g/2 oz chocolate chips

SAUCE

¾ cup/175 g/6 oz soft brown sugar

2 tbsp/25 g/1 oz butter

30 ml/2 tbsp golden syrup (or corn syrup)

60 ml/4 tbsp single cream (half and half or cereal cream)

PREPARATION

☛ Cream the butter or margarine and sugar together until light and fluffy.

☛ Gradually add the eggs, beating well between each addition.

☛ Sieve together the flour and cocoa, and fold into the egg mixture. Add enough milk to give a soft dropping consistency.

☛ Stir the banana and chocolate chips.

☛ Turn mixture into a greased 3¾ cup/900 ml/1½ pt pudding basin (bowl). Cover with greased grease-proof (waxed) paper and foil with a central pleat in each. Secure with string. Steam for about 1½ hours.

☛ To make the sauce, put all the ingredients into a saucepan and bring to the boil, stirring.

TO SERVE

Turn out pudding and serve with warm sauce.

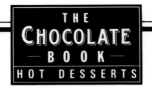
Magic Chocolate Pudding

INGREDIENTS

SERVES 4–5

1 cup + 2 tbsp/125 g/4 oz self-raising flour, sieved

¼ cup/50 g/2 oz sugar

30 ml/2 level tbsp unsweetened cocoa powder, sieved

⅓ cup/50 g/2 oz walnuts, chopped

4 tbsp/50 g/2 oz butter, melted

⅔ cup/150 ml/¼ pt milk

a few drops of vanilla essence (extract)

SAUCE

⅔ cup/150 g/5 oz soft brown sugar

30 ml/2 level tbsp unsweetened cocoa powder, sieved

a scant 1 cup/210 ml/¼ pt + 4 tbsp boiling water

oven temperature 180°C/350°F/Gas 4

PREPARATION

☛ To make the sponge, put the dry ingredients into a bowl. Add the butter, milk and essence and mix to form a thick batter.

☛ Pour the mixture into a buttered 7-in/900-ml/1½-pt ovenproof dish.

☛ To make the sauce, mix together the brown sugar, cocoa and boiling water. Pour this sauce over the batter.

☛ Bake in the oven for about 40 minutes. During cooking the chocolate sponge rises to the top, and a chocolate fudge sauce forms underneath.

TO SERVE

Accompany with vanilla ice cream.

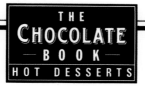
Chocolate Fondue

INGREDIENTS

SERVES 4–6

225 g/8 oz plain chocolate

225 g/8 oz milk chocolate

*1 cup/225 ml/8 fl oz single cream
(half and half or cereal cream)*

45 ml/3 tbsp Kahlua or Tia Maria

PREPARATION

☛ Break the chocolate into very small pieces into a heavy based saucepan. Add the cream and melt slowly over a low heat, stirring constantly.
☛ Immediately before serving, stir in the liqueur.

Small chunks of Madeira or other loaf cake, marshmallows, macaroons, whole strawberries, cherries, chunks of banana, pineapple and apple all make tasty dippers.

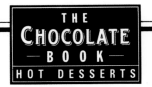

Chocolate Soufflé

INGREDIENTS

SERVES 4–6

4 tbsp/50 g/2 oz butter

½ cup/50 g/2 oz plain (all-purpose) flour

1¼ cup/300 ml/½ pt milk

¾ cup/75 g/3 oz plain chocolate, grated

3 eggs, separated

1 egg white

¼ cup/50 g/2 oz sugar

icing sugar

oven temperature 190°C/375°F/Gas 5

PREPARATION

☛ Melt the butter in a pan and stir in the flour. Remove from heat and stir in the milk. Return to heat and bring to the boil stirring. Cook gently for 2 minutes, stirring all the time.

☛ Remove from heat and stir in the chocolate.

☛ Beat in the egg yolks.

☛ Whisk all the egg whites until stiff. Whisk in the sugar a little at a time.

☛ Fold the chocolate sauce into the egg whites.

☛ Pour the mixture into a greased 8-in/1.2-l/2-pt soufflé dish.

☛ Bake in the oven for about 40 minutes until well risen and firm.

TO SERVE

Dredge with icing sugar.

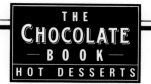
Baked Alaska

INGREDIENTS

SERVES 6 – 8

3¾ cups/900 ml/1½ pt chocolate ice cream

3 eggs

⅓ cup/75 g/3 oz sugar

scant ¾ cup/65 g/2½ oz plain (all-purpose) flour

30 ml/2 tbsp unsweetened cocoa powder

approximately 225 g/½ lb fruit (strawberries, bananas, raspberries, or cherries)

60 ml/4 tbsp Marsala or sweet sherry

4 egg whites

1 cup/225 g/8 oz sugar

*oven temperatures 200°C/400°F/Gas 6
and 230°C/450°F/Gas 8*

PREPARATION

☛ Pack the ice cream into a 450-g/1-lb loaf pan lined with non-stick (waxed) paper. Freeze overnight.

☛ Put the eggs and sugar into a bowl and whisk until thick and creamy, and the whisk leaves a trail.

☛ Sieve the flour and cocoa and fold gently into the mixture.

☛ Turn into a greased and lined 23-cm/9-in pan. Bake in the oven at the lower temperature for 12-15 minutes. Cool and remove paper.

☛ Prepare the fruit by slicing and removing stones if necessary. Put into a bowl with the Marsala or sherry.

☛ Whisk the egg whites until stiff. Whisk in the sugar a little at a time. Spoon the meringue into a piping bag fitted with a large star nozzle.

☛ Trim the edges of the sponge, then cut strips 2.5 cm/1 in from each of two sides of the cake to make an oblong slightly larger than the ice cream block.

☛ Put sponge on an ovenproof serving dish. Spoon the fruit and juices over the sponge.

☛ Remove the ice cream from the freezer and turn it onto the sponge. Remove the paper.

☛ Quickly pipe the meringue decoratively over the ice cream, covering it completely.

☛ Bake in the oven at the higher temperature for 3-5 minutes until lightly browned.

TO SERVE

Cut into slices and serve immediately.

Chocolate Upside-Down Pudding

INGREDIENTS

SERVES 6

½ cup/125 g/4 oz Demerara sugar

4 tbsp/50 g/2 oz butter

4 pineapple rings

6 walnut halves

2 eggs, separated

2 tbsp/25 g/1 oz butter, melted

½ cup/125 g/4 oz soft brown sugar

1 cup + 2 tbsp/125 g/4 oz self-raising flour

¼ cup/25 g/1 oz unsweetened cocoa powder

oven temperature 180°C/350°F/Gas 4

PREPARATION

☛ Grease a 20-cm/8-in cake pan.

☛ Cream together the sugar and butter and spread over the base of the pan. Arrange the pineapple rings on the base, with a walnut in the centre of each.

☛ Beat together the egg yolks and butter until creamy.

☛ Whisk the egg whites until stiff. Fold in the sugar and egg yolks mixture.

☛ Sieve together the flour and cocoa and fold in carefully. Pour over the fruit and spread evenly.

☛ Bake in the oven for about 30 minutes.

TO SERVE

Carefully turn out on to a serving dish and serve with pouring custard or single cream (cereal cream or half and half).

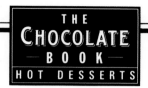
Cinnamon Chocolate Pain Perdu

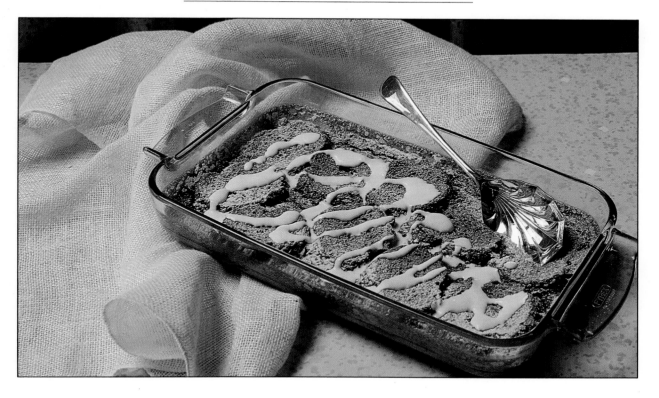

INGREDIENTS

SERVES 4–6

approximately ½ cup/75-125 g/3-4 oz butter

12-14 slices French bread

175 g/6 oz plain chocolate

2½ cups/600 ml/1 pt milk

2 eggs

2 egg yolks

5 ml/1 tsp ground cinnamon

¼ cup/50 g/2 oz sugar

icing sugar

oven temperature 190°C/375°F/Gas 5

PREPARATION

☛ Butter the slices of bread on both sides. Place on a baking tray and bake in the oven for about 5 minutes or until lightly golden. Turn over the bake on the other side until golden, about 2-5 minutes.

☛ Melt the chocolate.

☛ Bring the milk almost to boiling point. Remove from heat and whisk into the chocolate.

☛ Beat together the eggs, egg yolks, cinnamon and sugar. Pour on the chocolate milk and whisk well.

☛ Arrange the French bread in a large shallow baking dish. Strain the chocolate custard over the bread.

☛ Put the dish into a roasting pan and pour in boiling water to come half-way up the side of the baking dish.

☛ Cook in the oven for 30-40 minutes until lightly set.

TO SERVE

Dredge with icing sugar and serve with single cream (half and half or cereal cream).

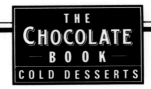
Cold Desserts

Chocolate Mousse

INGREDIENTS

SERVES 4–6

175 g/6 oz plain chocolate

30 ml/2 tbsp honey

3 eggs, separated

3 tsp/15 g/½ oz powdered gelatine (gelatin)

45 ml/3 tbsp hot water

⅔ cup/150 ml/¼ pt double (table) cream

TO SERVE

whipped cream

sliced bananas

PREPARATION

☛ Put chocolate and honey into a bowl over a pan of hot water and melt.

☛ Stir in egg yolks and beat until smooth. Remove from heat.

☛ Dissolve the gelatine in the water. Stir into the chocolate mixture. Chill until the mixture is the consistency of unbeaten egg white.

☛ Whip the cream until thick, but not stiff. Fold into the chocolate mixture.

☛ Whisk the egg whites until stiff and fold them into the chocolate mixture.

☛ Pour into an 8-in/1-l/1¾-pt mould. Chill until set.

☛ Unmould onto a serving dish.

TO SERVE

Pipe whipped cream round the base and decorate with banana slices.

Profiteroles

INGREDIENTS

SERVES 6

4 tbsp/50 g/2 oz unsalted butter

⅔ cup/150 ml/¼ pt water

⅔ cup/65 g/2½ oz plain (all-purpose) flour

2 eggs, beaten

FILLING

1¼ cups/300 ml/½ pt double (table) cream

¼ cup/25 g/1 oz icing sugar, sieved

a little Grand Marnier

10 ml/2 tsp finely-grated orange rind

CHOCOLATE SAUCE

125 g/4 oz plain chocolate

30 ml/2 tbsp orange juice

½ cup/50 g/2 oz icing sugar

2 tbsp/25 g/1 oz butter

oven temperature 200°C/400°F/Gas 6

PREPARATION

☞ Melt the butter in a pan with the water.
☞ Bring to the boil and immediately tip in the flour. Beat well until the mixture forms a ball that comes cleanly away from the pan. Leave to cool.
☞ Beat or whisk in the eggs, a little at a time. Continue beating until the mixture is smooth and glossy.
☞ Put mixture into a piping bag fitted with a 1.25-cm/½-in plain nozzle. Pipe about 24 small balls on to a greased and floured baking sheet.
☞ Bake in the oven for 15–20 minutes until well risen and golden brown. A few minutes before removing from the oven, pierce them with a sharp knife to release the steam. Cool on a wire rack.
☞ To make the filling, whisk the cream until stiff. Stir in the icing sugar, Grand Marnier and orange rind. Put the cream in a piping bag fitted with a small nozzle and pipe the cream into the choux buns through the slits.
☞ To make the sauce, put all the ingredients into a bowl over a pan of hot water and heat until melted. Stir well together.

TO SERVE

Pile the profiteroles on a serving dish and just before serving, pour over the warm sauce.

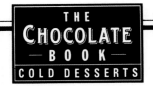
Charlotte Louise

INGREDIENTS

SERVES 8

18-20 sponge fingers

¾ cup/175 g/6 oz unsalted butter

⅓ cup/75 g/3 oz sugar

175 g/6 oz plain chocolate

1 cup/125 g/4 oz ground almonds

1¼ cups/300 ml/½ pt double (table) cream

2.5 ml/½ tsp almond essence (extract)

DECORATION

whipped cream

pistachio nuts

crystallized violets or roses

satin ribbon

PREPARATION

☞ Cut a round of greaseproof (waxed) paper to fit the base of an 8- or 9-in/1.4-l/2½-pt Charlotte mould. Oil it lightly and place in the mould.

☞ Line the sides of the mould with the sponge fingers.

☞ Cream the butter and sugar together until light and fluffy.

☞ Melt the chocolate. Cool slightly, then beat into the butter together with the ground almonds.

☞ Whip the cream until thick, but not stiff. Add the almond essence. Fold into the chocolate mixture and mix well.

☞ Spoon mixture into the lined mould. Press in firmly.

☞ Chill well.

TO SERVE

Turn out on to a plate. Remove paper and pipe with whipped cream. Decorate with pistachio nuts and violets. Tie a satin ribbon around the Charlotte.

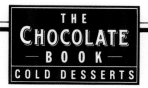

Pears and Chocolate Sauce

INGREDIENTS

SERVES 6

125 g/4 oz plain chocolate

30 ml/2 tbsp strong black coffee

30 ml/2 tbsp apricot jam

45 ml/3 tbsp water

60 ml/4 tbsp double (table) cream

a large pinch of ground cinnamon

4-8 scoops vanilla or chocolate ice cream

6 ripe pears, peeled, halved and cored

TO SERVE

crisp biscuits (cookies) (such as Langues de chat)

PREPARATION

☛ Put the chocolate, coffee, jam and water into a small heavy pan. Slowly bring to the boil, stirring constantly.

☛ Remove from heat and stir in cream and cinnamon.

☛ Sieve into a bowl and leave to cool.

☛ Put 1 or 2 scoops of ice cream in 6 individual serving dishes. Arrange 2 pear halves on each serving.

TO SERVE

Spoon over the chocolate sauce and serve immediately with crisp biscuits.

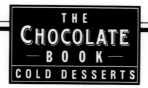
Chocolate Orange Pots

INGREDIENTS

SERVES 8

175 g/6 oz plain chocolate

rind of 1 small orange, finely grated

3 eggs, separated

30-45 ml/2-3 tbsp orange Curaçao

1 cup/225 ml/8 fl oz double (table) cream

DECORATION

whipped cream

orange rind spirals

chocolate orange sticks

PREPARATION

☞ Put chocolate into a bowl over a pan of hot water and melt.

☞ Remove from heat and stir in the orange rind, egg yolks and liqueur. Stir well and leave to cool.

☞ Whip cream until thick. Whisk egg whites until stiff. Fold cream and egg whites into the chocolate mixture.

☞ Pour into 8 individual pots (e.g. custard cups) and chill well.

TO SERVE

Top with a spoonful of softly whipped cream and decorate with orange rind spirals and chocolate sticks.

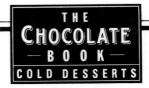

Snowball Pie

SERVES 6

225 g/8 oz plain chocolate

1 tbsp/50 g/2 oz butter

½ cup/75 g/3 oz crisp rice cereal (Rice Krispies)

2 cups/400 ml/¾ pt vanilla ice cream

2 cups/400 ml/¾ pt chocolate ice cream

2 cups/400 ml/¾ pt strawberry ice cream

TO SERVE

Chocolate or Fudge Sauce (see page 116)

long shred coconut, toasted

PREPARATION

☞ Melt the chocolate and butter together.
☞ Stir in the crisp rice cereal and mix well together.
☞ Press the mixture over the base and up the sides of a 20-cm/8-in flan dish (pie plate). Place in the freezer until firm.
☞ Arrange alternate scoops of the ice cream.
☞ Pour over the sauce and sprinkle with the coconut. Serve immediately.

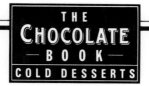
Chocolate Trifle

INGREDIENTS

SERVES 6

200 g/7 oz chocolate Swiss roll (jelly roll)

approx 2 cups/420-g/14-oz can apricot halves, drained

2½ cups/600 ml/1 pt Chocolate Custard (see page 115)

1¼ cups/300 ml/½ pt double (table) cream, whipped

DECORATION

Chocolate Heart Cut-outs (see page 18)

ratafias

glacé cherries, etc

PREPARATION

☛ Cut the Swiss roll into 1-cm/½-in slices and arrange over the base and sides of a trifle dish.

☛ Arrange the drained apricots on top.

☛ Pour the cold Chocolate Custard over the apricots.

☛ Pipe the whipped double cream over the top. Decorate with Chocolate Hearts, etc, as desired.

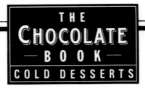

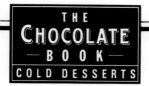
Chocolate Ice Cream

INGREDIENTS

SERVES 4–6

¾ cup/175 g/6 oz sugar

⅔ cup/150 ml/¼ pt water

450 g/1 lb plain or milk chocolate

4 egg yolks

3¾ cups/900 ml/1½ pt double (table) cream

PREPARATION

☛ Put sugar and water into a saucepan and stir over a gentle heat until dissolved. Bring to the boil and simmer gently for 7 minutes.

☛ Break the chocolate into small pieces and stir into the hot syrup. Stir until dissolved.

☛ Whisk in the egg yolks. Cool.

☛ Whip the cream until thick, but not stiff. Fold into the chocolate mixture.

☛ Freeze in an electric ice cream maker according to manufacturer's instructions. Alternatively, pour into a freezer tray and freeze. Beat the mixture twice, at hourly intervals. Cover, seal and freeze.

TO SERVE

Remove ice cream from freezer to refrigerator and allow to 'come to' about 30 minutes before serving.

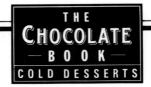
Chocolate Roulade

INGREDIENTS

SERVES 6-8

175 g/6 oz plain chocolate

5 eggs, separated

¾ cup/175 g/6 oz sugar

45 ml/3 tbsp hot water

icing sugar, sieved

FILLING

2 cups/425 ml/¾ pt double (table) cream

½ cup/50 g/2 oz icing sugar, sieved

¼ cup/25 g/1 oz unsweetened cocoa powder

10 ml/2 tsp instant coffee

2.5 ml/½ tsp vanilla essence (extract)

DECORATION

icing sugar

whipped cream

crystallized violets

angelica leaves

oven temperature 180°C/350°F/Gas 4

PREPARATION

☛ Melt the chocolate in a bowl over a pan of hot water.
☛ Put egg yolks into a large bowl. Add the sugar and beat well until pale and fluffy.
☛ Add hot water to the chocolate and stir until smooth. Whisk into the egg mixture.
☛ Whisk the egg whites until stiff. Lightly fold into the chocolate mixture. Pour into a greased and lined 39 × 24 cm/15½ × 9½ in Swiss roll (jelly roll) pan.
☛ Cook in the oven for 15-20 minutes, until firm.
☛ Remove from the oven. Cover with a sheet of greaseproof or waxed paper and a damp tea-towel. Leave until completely cold.
☛ To make the filling put all the ingredients into a bowl. Whisk until thick. Chill.
☛ Turn roulade on to a sheet of greaseproof (waxed) paper dusted with icing sugar. Peel away lining paper.
☛ Spread the filling over the roulade to within 2.5 cm/1 in from the edge. Roll up like a Swiss roll, using the greaseproof paper to help.
☛ Place seam side down on a serving plate and chill for one hour before serving.

TO SERVE

Dredge the roulade with icing sugar. Pipe whipped cream down the centre and decorate with crystallized violets and angelica leaves.

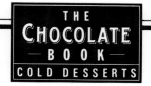
Chocolate Cheesecake Cups

INGREDIENTS

SERVES 6

approx 2¾ cups/450 g/1 lb cream cheese

3 eggs, separated

½ cup/125 g/4 oz sugar

⅔ cup/150 ml/¼ pt sour cream

2 tbsp/15 g/½ oz powdered gelatine (gelatin)

60 ml/4 tbsp water

¾ cup/175 g/6 oz plain or milk chocolate, chopped

175 g/6 oz plain chocolate

6 individual shortcrust pastry cases (tart shells)
(approx 7.5 cm/3 in diameter)

DECORATION

Chocolate Caraque (see page 17)

PREPARATION

☛ Put the cheese and egg yolks into a bowl. Add half of the sugar and beat well together.
☛ Stir in the sour cream.
☛ Dissolve the gelatine in the water.
☛ Whisk the egg whites until stiff. Whisk in the remaining sugar.
☛ Stir the gelatine into the cheese mixture.
☛ Fold the meringue and the chopped chocolate into the cheese mixture.
☛ Pour into six individual moulds and chill until set.
☛ Melt the chocolate and spread over the underneath and outsides of the pastry cases. Place upside down over small glasses to set.
☛ Turn out the cheesecakes and place one in each chocolate cup.

TO SERVE

Decorate with Chocolate Caraque.

Chocolate and Coffee Bavarois

INGREDIENTS

SERVES 6–8
4 egg yolks
¼ cup/50 g/2 oz sugar
5 ml/1 tsp vanilla essence (extract)
2½ cups/568 ml/1 pt milk
1½ cups/175 g/6 oz plain chocolate, grated
15 ml/1 tbsp coffee essence (eg Camp)
2 tbsp/15 g/½ oz powdered gelatine (gelatin)
60 ml/4 tbsp cold water
⅔ cup/150 ml/¼ pt double (table) cream
⅓ cup/150 ml/¼ pt single (half and half or cereal) cream
2 egg whites

DECORATION
whipped cream
Chocolate Caraque (see page 17)

PREPARATION

☛ Beat together the egg yolks, sugar and vanilla essence until pale and fluffy.

☛ Warm the milk. Stir into the egg yolk mixture. Put into a double saucepan or a bowl over a pan of hot water. Stir gently until the mixture thickens.

☛ Stir the chocolate and coffee essence into the custard. Stir until completely dissolved. Remove from heat.

☛ Put water into a bowl and add the gelatine. Place over a pan of hot water and stir until dissolved. Cool slightly.

☛ Stir the gelatine into the chocolate custard. Leave until the mixture begins to thicken.

☛ Whisk the creams together until thick. Whisk the egg whites until stiff.

☛ Fold the cream into the chocolate mixture.

☛ Fold the egg whites into the mixture thoroughly.

☛ Pour into a lightly-oiled approx 8-in/1.5-l/2½-pt mould. Chill until set.

TO SERVE

Turn Bavarois out on to a serving plate. Decorate with piped whipped cream and Chocolate Caraque.

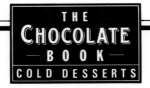

Chocolate Hazelnut Bombe

INGREDIENTS

SERVES 6-8

2½ cups/600 ml/1 pt vanilla ice cream

⅓ cup/50 g/2 oz hazelnuts, finely chopped and toasted

2½ cups/600 ml/1 pt Chocolate Ice Cream (see page 87)

30 ml/2 tbsp dark rum

DECORATION

1¼ cups/300 ml/½ pt double (table) cream, whipped

whole hazelnuts

PREPARATION

☛ Put an 8- or 9-in/1.2-l/2-pt bombe mould or pudding basin (bowl) into the freezer overnight.
☛ Soften the vanilla ice cream and mix in the hazelnuts. Line the bombe mould with the ice cream and freeze.
☛ Soften the chocolate ice cream and blend in the rum. Fill the centre of the bombe. Cover with oiled greaseproof or waxed paper and freeze.

TO SERVE

Turn out the bombe on to a plate. Pipe with whipped cream and decorate with whole hazelnuts. Serve cut into wedges.

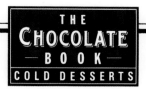

Choc-Chestnut Mont Blanc

INGREDIENTS

SERVES 6-8

4 tbsp/50 g/2 oz unsalted butter

25 g/1 oz sugar

175 g/6 oz plain chocolate, melted

2 cups/350 g/12 oz chestnut purée

15-30 ml/1-2 tbsp sherry

DECORATION

whipped cream

ratafias

glacé chestnuts

grated chocolate

PREPARATION

☛ Cream the butter and sugar together until light and fluffy.

☛ Beat in the melted chocolate.

☛ Blend in the chestnut purée and sherry.

☛ Pile the mixture into the centre of individual dessert dishes and form into mountain shapes. Chill.

☛ Spoon or pipe a capping of whipped cream on the summit. Decorate the base with ratafia biscuits and glacé chestnuts. Sprinkle with grated chocolate if you wish.

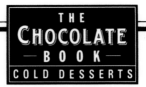
Mohr Im Hemd (Moor In His Nightshirt)

INGREDIENTS

SERVES 6-8

½ cup/125 g/4 oz butter

½ cup/125 g/4 oz sugar

6 eggs, separated

1 cup/125 g/4 oz plain chocolate, grated

¾ cup/125 g/4 oz ground almonds

5 ml/1 tsp coffee essence (extract)

SAUCE

175 g/6 oz plain chocolate

¾ cup/175 ml/6 fl oz water

6 tbsp/75 g/3 oz unsalted butter

CREAM

⅔ cup/150 ml/¼ pt single (half and half or cereal) cream

⅔ cup/150 ml/¼ pt double (table) cream

15-30 ml/1-2 tbsp icing sugar

a few drops of vanilla essence (extract)

oven temperature 180°C/350°F/Gas 4

PREPARATION

☛ Cream together the butter and sugar until light and fluffy. Beat in the egg yolks one at a time.

☛ Mix in the chocolate, almonds and essence.

☛ Whisk the egg whites until stiff and fold gently into the chocolate mixture.

☛ Butter and dust with caster sugar 6–8 individual ovenproof soufflé dishes. Pour in the chocolate mixture.

☛ Place in a roasting pan, half filled with hot water. Bake in the oven for 30–40 minutes until puffed and just firm. Leave to cool for a few minutes.

☛ To make the sauce put the chocolate and water into a pan. Stir over a low heat until the mixture is smooth. Remove from the heat and stir in the butter.

☛ Whisk the single and double creams together until light and fluffy. Stir in the icing sugar and vanilla essence.

☛ Spoon a little sauce on to each serving plate. Invert the puddings onto the sauce. Cover puddings with whipped cream.

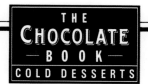

Chocolate Terrine

INGREDIENTS

SERVES 6–8

one purchased 450-g/1-lb Madeira or other loaf cake

175 g/6 oz plain chocolate

²/₃ cup/150 g/5 oz sugar

60 ml/4 tbsp water

1 cup/125 g/4 oz cocoa

¾ cup/175 g/6 oz unsalted butter

1 egg

2 egg yolks

¼ cup/50 g/2 oz glacé cherries, chopped

⅓ cup/50 g/2 oz raisins

⅓ cup/50 g/2 oz pistachios, chopped

1¼ cups/300 ml/½ pt whipping cream

PREPARATION

☛ Line a 1.2–kg/3–lb loaf pan with non-stick (waxed) paper).

☛ Cut the loaf cake into thin slices. Line the bottom and sides of pan with some slices.

☛ Melt the chocolate.

☛ Put the sugar and water into a small pan and heat gently over a low heat until the sugar is dissolved.

☛ Beat together the cocoa and butter. Beat in the sugar syrup, melted chocolate and eggs. Stir in the cherries, raisins and pistachios.

☛ Spread one third of the chocolate mixture in the lined pan. Top with slices of cake. Continue in this way, ending with a layer of cake. Trim cake level. Cover and chill overnight.

☛ Unmould terrine onto a serving plate and spread the whipped cream over the top and sides of terrine.

Kids' Recipes

Chocolate Peppermint Creams

INGREDIENTS

MAKES ABOUT 40

1 large egg white

1.25 ml/¼ tsp peppermint essence

a few drops green or pink food colouring (optional)

2½ cups/350 g/12 oz icing sugar, sieved

a little cornflour (cornstarch)

125 g/4 oz plain or milk chocolate

PREPARATION

☛ Put egg white, essence and colouring into a bowl.

☛ Gradually stir in the icing sugar until a stiff paste is formed. Knead until smooth.

☛ Lightly dust a board with cornflour. Roll out to about 0.75 cm/¼ in thick. Using 4-cm/1½-in fancy cutters (fluted, hearts, diamonds, etc) stamp out shapes and place on non-stick paper. Leave to dry overnight.

☛ Melt the chocolate. Dip each sweet in the chocolate so only half is coated. Shake off any drips. Place on non-stick or waxed paper and leave to set.

Chocolate Easter Nests

INGREDIENTS

MAKES ABOUT 6

1 Shredded Wheat

1 cup cornflakes

⅓ cup/75 g/3 oz plain chocolate, broken in pieces

15 ml/1 tbsp butter

15 ml/1 tbsp golden syrup

15 ml/1 tbsp sugar

15 ml/1 tbsp unsweetened cocoa powder

miniature sugar eggs

PREPARATION

☛ Break up the Shredded Wheat. Lightly crush the cornflakes. Put both into a bowl.

☛ Put the chocolate, butter, syrup, sugar and cocoa into a saucepan. Melt gently together. Stir well.

☛ Pour over the Shredded Wheat and cornflakes and mix well together.

☛ Spoon into foil tartlet cases or paper cake cases (cupcake papers) and shape into nests with a teaspoon.

☛ Put in the fridge to set.

TO SERVE

Fill each nest with a few miniature sugar (Easter) eggs.

Frozen Chocolate Sandwiches

INGREDIENTS

MAKES ABOUT 20

½ cup/125 g/4 oz butter

½ cup/125 g/4 oz sugar

30 ml/2 tbsp beaten egg

a few drops vanilla essence (extract)

¼ cup/25 g/1 oz unsweetened cocoa powder

1¾ cups/200 g/7 oz plain (all-purpose) flour

FILLING

1 large egg white

90 ml/6 tbsp sugar

1 cup/225 ml/8 fl oz double (table) cream

15 ml/1 tbsp unsweetened cocoa powder

a few drops of vanilla essence (extract)

COATING

Chopped toasted almonds, alternatively toasted desiccated (shredded) coconut or crushed digestive biscuits (Graham wafers)

oven temperature 180°C/350°F/Gas 4

PREPARATION

☛ Beat the butter and sugar until pale and creamy.

☛ Beat in the egg and vanilla essence.

☛ Stir in the flour and cocoa, which have been sieved together, to give a firm dough.

☛ Knead lightly until smooth. Roll out on a lightly floured surface to a thickness of about 0.5 cm/¼ in.

☛ Using a 6.5-cm/2½-in round fluted cutter, stamp out circles.

☛ Put on a baking sheet and cook in the oven for about 15 minutes. Cool on a wire rack.

☛ To make the filling, whisk the egg white until stiff. Whisk in 30 ml/2 tbsp of the sugar.

☛ Put cream, remaining sugar, cocoa and vanilla essence into another bowl and whisk until stiff.

☛ Fold egg white into chocolate mixture.

☛ Put a spoonful of the mixture on to half the chocolate biscuits. Top with remaining biscuits. Press lightly so filling reaches the edges.

☛ Arrange on a baking sheet and freeze until firm.

☛ Spread the chosen coating on a baking sheet. Run each sandwich through the coating like a wheel, so that the sides are covered.

☛ Wrap individually in foil and freeze overnight.

"Christmas Pudding" Cakes

INGREDIENTS

MAKES 4–6

125 g/4 oz plain chocolate

30 ml/2 tbsp butter

30 ml/2 tbsp orange juice

30 ml/2 tbsp icing sugar

30 ml/2 tbsp cake crumbs (preferably a plain sponge)

15 ml/1 tbsp ground almonds

DECORATION

grated chocolate

a little thick white glacé icing

glacé cherries

angelica leaves

PREPARATION

☛ Melt the chocolate in a bowl over a pan of hot water.

☛ Stir in the butter until melted. Remove from heat.

☛ Stir in the orange juice, icing sugar, cake crumbs and ground almonds. Mix well.

☛ Chill for about 1 hour until firm.

☛ Roll into balls and coat in the grated chocolate.

☛ Put into small paper cake cases (cupcake papers). Top with a little thick glacé icing and decorate with pieces of glacé cherry and angelica leaves.

Sweetmeats

Amaretti Truffles

INGREDIENTS

MAKES ABOUT 16

4 tbsp/50 g/2 oz butter

1 cup/175 g/6 oz icing sugar

75 g/3 oz plain chocolate

5 ml/1 tsp instant coffee

a few drops of almond essence (extract)

approx 16 small, hard macaroons
(preferably Italian Amaretti)

125 g/4 oz plain chocolate

PREPARATION

☛ Beat together the butter and icing sugar.
☛ Put the chocolate into a bowl over a pan of hot water. Dissolve the coffee in a few drops of boiling water and add to the chocolate. Heat until melted.
☛ Remove chocolate from heat and add the essence. Stir into the butter mixture. Chill until firm enough to handle.
☛ Roll mixture into balls and press each one on to the flat side of a macaroon.
☛ Melt the chocolate and dip each 'truffle' side of the macaroons. Leave to set, coated sides up.

Colettes

INGREDIENTS

MAKES ABOUT 16

225 g/8 oz plain chocolate

15 ml/1 tbsp strong black coffee

30 ml/2 tbsp single (half and half or cereal) cream

4 tbsp/50 g/2 oz butter

2 egg yolks

10-15 ml/2-3 tsp dark rum (or brandy, sherry, Cointreau or Maraschino)

DECORATION

small pieces of nuts, cherries, or crystallized flowers

PREPARATION

☛ Melt half the chocolate. Use double layers of paper petit fours cases, or preferably single foil petit fours cases. Spoon a little chocolate into each case. With the handle of a teaspoon, spread evenly around the base and sides of each case.

☛ Turn upside down on to a tray lined with non-stick or waxed paper and leave to set in a cool place.

☛ Melt the remaining chocolate in a bowl over a pan of hot water. Add the coffee and cream and stir.

☛ Remove from the heat. Dice the butter. Beat into the chocolate mixture a little at a time.

☛ Beat in the egg yolks and rum. Leave in a cool place until thick.

☛ Carefully peel the cases away from the chocolate. Using a piping bag fitted with a star nozzle, pipe the filling into each case.

☛ Top with the decoration of your choice. Place in clean paper cases, or a decorative box.

Rich Chocolate Truffles

INGREDIENTS

MAKES ABOUT 30

225 g/8 oz plain or milk chocolate

½ cup/125 g/4 oz butter, diced

10 ml/2 tsp liqueur (eg Tia Maria, Cointreau,
rum or brandy)

1 cup/175 g/6 oz icing sugar

COATING

ground nuts

PREPARATION

☛ Melt the chocolate. Remove from heat.
☛ Add the butter and liqueur and beat until smooth.
☛ Beat in the icing sugar.
☛ Chill well until firm.
☛ Shape into 2.5-cm/1-in balls and roll in the nuts.

TO SERVE

Place in paper cases (cupcake papers) and keep cool.

VARIATIONS

The truffles could also be coated in icing sugar, cocoa
powder, drinking chocolate powder, ground praline
or grated chocolate.

Rocky Road Fudge

INGREDIENTS

MAKES ABOUT 700 G / 1 ½ LB

450 g/1 lb milk chocolate

4 tbsp/50 g/2 oz butter

30 ml/2 tbsp single (half and half or cereal) cream

5 ml/1 tsp vanilla essence (extract)

⅓ cup/50 g/2 oz walnuts, chopped

approx 2 cups/125 g/4 oz marshmallows, cut into small pieces with wetted scissors

1 cup/225 g/8 oz icing sugar, sieved

DECORATION

75 g/3 oz plain chocolate

PREPARATION

☛ Melt the chocolate and butter in a bowl over a pan of hot water. Stir in the cream and essence.
☛ Remove from heat and stir in the walnuts, marshmallows and icing sugar.
☛ Spread in a 20-cm/8-in square pan, lined with non-stick (waxed) paper.
☛ Chill until firm.
☛ Melt the plain chocolate. Using a piping bag fitted with a plain nozzle, drizzle the chocolate over the fudge. Leave to set.

TO SERVE

Cut the fudge into diamond shapes.

Chocolate Fudge

INGREDIENTS

MAKES ABOUT 700 G / 1½ LB

2 cups/450 g/1 lb sugar

⅔ cup/150 ml/¼ pt milk

½ cup/125 g/4 oz butter

175 g/6 oz plain chocolate

scant ¼ cup/50 g/2 oz honey

PREPARATION

☛ Put all the ingredients into a heavy based saucepan.
☛ Stir continuously over a gentle heat until the sugar is completely dissolved.
☛ Bring to the boil and cook to the 'soft ball' stage, 116°C/240°F.
☛ Remove from heat and dip the base of the pan in cold water to stop further cooking.
☛ Leave for 5 minutes. Then beat the mixture with a wooden spoon until thick and creamy and beginning to 'grain.' Before it becomes too stiff, pour into a buttered 20-cm/8-in square pan. Leave to set.
☛ Using a greased knife, cut into 2.5-cm/1-in squares. To store fudge, put in a tin between layers of non-stick (waxed) paper.

Chocolate Eggs

INGREDIENTS

MAKES 4

4 medium eggs

225 g/8 oz plain or milk chocolate

½ cup/75 g/3 oz praline, ground finely

30 ml/2 tbsp cream

PREPARATION

☛ Using an egg prick or pin, pierce a hole at the pointed end of each egg.

☛ Using small scissors, carefully enlarge the hole to about 1 cm/½ in.

☛ Using a cocktail stick or toothpick, push it into the hole to puncture the yolk. Shake the raw egg into a bowl.

☛ Run water gently into the shells and shake until they are clean. Turn upside down and leave to dry.

☛ Melt the chocolate. Stir in the praline and cream. Spoon or pour the chocolate into the dry shells. Leave until set.

☛ Seal the holes with small round labels and place in an egg box, hole side down.

VARIATIONS

Alternatively, when the chocolate has set, gently tap and peel away the shell. Pipe royal icing, or melted chocolate in decorative patterns onto the eggs. Decorate with silver balls, icing flowers, ribbons, etc.

If intended for adults, a little brandy or rum can be added to the chocolate.

109

Chocolate Dipped Fruits

INGREDIENTS

*450 g/1 lb fruit (eg strawberries, grapes, cherries,
mandarin segments, peeled lychees)*

450 g/1 lb plain chocolate

PREPARATION

☛ Make sure the fruit is firm. Wash and dry well,
leaving on stalks where applicable.

☛ Melt the chocolate.

☛ Holding the fruit by the stem, or using a cocktail
stick or toothpick, dip it half-way into the chocolate.
Leave the top half uncovered. Shake off the excess
chocolate.

☛ Place the fruit on a tray lined with non-stick or
waxed paper and leave in a cool place to dry.

TO SERVE

Put dipped fruits into petit fours cases and serve
within 24 hours.

VARIATIONS

Crystallized orange peel, crystallized ginger, and
pineapple may also be dipped in this way. These will
also keep for longer, so are better for present giving.

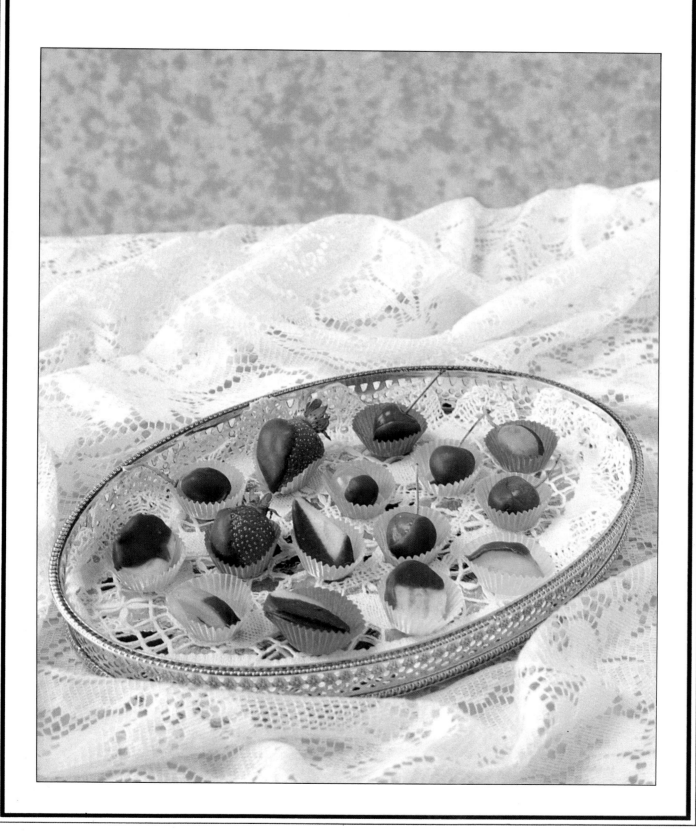

Meringue Mushrooms

INGREDIENTS

MAKES ABOUT 8

1 egg white

¼ cup/50 g/2 oz caster sugar

50 g/2 oz plain chocolate, melted

TO SERVE

unsweetened cocoa powder

oven temperature 140°C/275°F/Gas 1

PREPARATION

☛ Whisk the egg white until stiff.
☛ Whisk in the sugar a little at a time until the mixture is stiff and glossy.
☛ Put meringue into a piping bag fitted with a 1 cm/½ in plain nozzle.
☛ Line a baking sheet with non-stick (waxed) paper. Pipe 6–8 small mounds of meringue about 2.5 cm/1 in in diameter to form the mushroom caps.
☛ Next pipe 6–8 smaller mounds, drawing each one up to a point, to represent the stalks.
☛ Bake in the oven for about 1 hour until dry and crisp. Allow to cool.
☛ Using the point of a sharp knife, make a tiny hole in the base of each mushroom cap.
☛ Spread a little melted chocolate on the underside of each cap and gently push on a stalk. Allow to set.
☛ Before using, dust the tops of mushrooms with a little cocoa powder.

Chocolate Caramel Popcorn

INGREDIENTS

¼ cup/50 g/2 oz brown sugar

2 tbsp/25 g/1 oz butter

25 ml/1½ tbsp golden syrup (or corn syrup)

15 ml/1 tbsp milk

¼ cup/50 g/2 oz chocolate chips

a pinch of bicarbonate of soda (baking soda)

5 cups/1.1 l/2 pt popped popcorn

oven temperature 150°C/300°F/Gas 2

PREPARATION

☛ Put the sugar, butter, syrup and milk into a heavy-based saucepan.

☛ Stir over a gentle heat until the butter and sugar have melted. Bring to the boil.

☛ Boil without stirring for 2 minutes.

☛ Remove from heat. Add chocolate and bicarbonate of soda. Stir until the chocolate is melted.

☛ Measure the popped popcorn into a bowl. Pour over the syrup and toss well until evenly coated.

☛ Spread mixture on a large baking tray. Bake in the oven for about 15 minutes. Test for crispness. Bake for a further 5-10 minutes if necessary. Cool.

Sauces

Tobler Sauce

INGREDIENTS

SERVES 4

225 g/8 oz Toblerone Chocolate

⅔ cup/150 ml/¼ pt double (table) cream

PREPARATION

☛ Cut chocolate into very small pieces. Put into a small pan and melt very quickly.

☛ Stir in the cream. Mix until smooth and immediately pour over ice cream or fruit such as bananas or pears, etc.

Chocolate Sauce

INGREDIENTS

SERVES 3-4

½ cup/50 g/2 oz unsweetened cocoa powder

60 ml/4 tbsp golden syrup

4 tbsp/50 g/2 oz butter

⅔ cup/150 ml/¼ pt milk

2.5 ml/½ tsp vanilla essence (extract)

PREPARATION

☛ Put cocoa, golden syrup and butter into a small pan. Heat gently until well blended.

☛ Stir in the milk and essence.

☛ Bring to the boil and simmer gently for about 3 minutes. Serve hot or cold.

VARIATIONS

Chocolate/Orange Sauce: Omit vanilla essence Add grated rind of ½ orange.

Honey Chocolate Sauce: Use clear honey instead of golden syrup. Add lemon juice instead of vanilla essence.

Choco-Nutty Sauce: Omit vanilla essence. Stir in 15 ml/1 tbsp peanut butter.

Choco-Ginger Sauce: Add ¼ cup/25 g/1 oz chopped stem ginger.

Fudge Sauce

INGREDIENTS

SERVES 4-6

15 ml/1 tbsp unsweetened cocoa powder

¾ cup/175-g/6-oz can evaporated milk

¾ cup/75 g/3 oz plain chocolate, grated

2 tbsp/25 g/1 oz butter

2 tbsp/25 g/1 oz soft brown sugar

PREPARATION

☛ Put cocoa and evaporated milk into a pan and whisk well together.

☛ Add all the remaining ingredients. Heat gently, stirring until the chocolate, sugar and butter have melted. Do not boil. Serve hot or warm.

Chocolate Syrup

FUDGE SAUCE

CHOCOLATE SAUCE

CHOCOLATE SYRUP

This syrup can be used for milk shakes, to pour over ice cream, pancakes, waffles, etc. To thin it just add a little cream or milk.

INGREDIENTS

1½ cups/350 g/12 oz soft brown sugar
1 cup/125 g/4 oz unsweetened cocoa
1¼ cups/300 ml/½ pt boiling water
10 ml/2 tsp vanilla essence (extract)

PREPARATION

☛ Mix together the sugar and cocoa.
☛ Add the water, stirring continuously.
☛ Put mixture into a small pan and simmer gently for 5 minutes, stirring frequently.
☛ Cool. Add vanilla essence.
☛ Cover and chill in the refrigerator.

Chocolate Custard

INGREDIENTS

MAKES 2½ CUPS 600 ML/1 PT

2½ cups/600 ml/1 pt milk

6 egg yolks

¼ cup/50 g/2 oz sugar

1 cup/125 g/4 oz plain chocolate, grated

PREPARATION

☛ Put milk into a saucepan and bring almost to the boil. Remove from the heat.
☛ Whisk the egg yolks and sugar together until thick and fluffy.
☛ Gradually pour the milk on to the eggs and sugar, whisking continuously.
☛ Return mixture to saucepan and stir over a very gentle heat, until it coats the back of a spoon.
☛ Remove from heat and add the chocolate. Stir until dissolved.

TO SERVE

Serve the custard hot or cold.

To cool the custard, pour into a bowl and place dampened greaseproof or waxed paper directly on to the surface to stop a 'skin' from forming. Chill.

Mars Bar Sauce

Both this and the Tobler Sauce recipe (see page 119) are very quick to make and absolutely delicious.

INGREDIENTS

SERVES 4

4 Mars Bars

90 ml/6 tbsp double (table) cream

PREPARATION

☛ Dice the Mars Bars. Put in a small pan and melt very gently.

☛ Stir in the cream. Mix until smooth and immediately pour over ice cream.

VARIATIONS

☛ For extra punch, add a little brandy or rum to taste.

Drinks

Hot Chocolate

INGREDIENTS

225 g/8 oz plain chocolate

1¼ cups/300 ml/½ pt water

2 cups/450 ml/¾ pt milk

TO SERVE

brown sugar

marshmallows or whipped cream

drinking chocolate powder

PREPARATION

☛ Put the chocolate and water into a pan. Heat gently, stirring until dissolved.
☛ Heat the milk just to boiling.
☛ Pour the hot milk on to the chocolate and whisk until frothy.

TO SERVE

Pour into hot mugs. Add brown sugar if desired. Top with marshmallows or a dollop of whipped cream. Sprinkle with drinking chocolate powder.

Iced Caribbean Chocolate

INGREDIENTS

SERVES 4

2 cups/400 ml/¾ pt milk

⅔ cup/150 ml/¼ pt single (half and half or cereal) cream

2 large pinches of ground nutmeg

2 large pinches of ground cinnamon

a large pinch of ground allspice

75 ml/5 tbsp Chocolate Syrup (see page 117)

TO SERVE

coffee ice cream

ice cubes

PREPARATION

☛ Put the milk, cream, spices and syrup into a bowl and whisk well together. Chill well.
☛ Before serving, whisk again.

TO SERVE

Pour into glasses over ice cubes and top with scoops of coffee ice cream.

Choconana Milk Shake

INGREDIENTS

SERVES 2-3

1¼ cups/300 ml/½ pt milk

45 ml/3 tbsp Chocolate Syrup (see page 117)

2½ cups/600 ml/1 pt chocolate ice cream

1 banana, cut into pieces

TO SERVE

bought chocolate flake bars

PREPARATION

☛ Put milk, chocolate syrup, ice cream and banana into a blender.
☛ Cover and blend until smooth.

TO SERVE

Pour into glasses and add a chocolate flake to each one.

ICED CARIBBEAN CHOCOLATE

CHOCONANA MILK SHAKE

Chocolate Egg Nog

INGREDIENTS

SERVES 4-6

2 eggs

30 ml/2 tbsp sugar

approx 1 cup/200 ml/⅓ pt milk

45 ml/3 tbsp Chocolate Syrup (see page 117)

30 ml/2 tbsp Crème de Cacao

30 ml/2 tbsp Amaretto

a few drops of vanilla essence (extract)

approx 1 cup/200 ml/⅓ pt whipping cream

grated nutmeg

PREPARATION

☛ Separate the eggs.

☛ Put egg yolks and 15 ml/1 tbsp of sugar into a bowl and whisk until thick and pale.

☛ Add milk, chocolate syrup, liqueurs and essence, and whisk well. Chill.

☛ Whisk the whipping cream until loosely thick (NOT stiff). Whisk the egg whites until stiff and fold in the remaining sugar.

☛ Stir the egg yolk mixture into the whipped cream.

☛ Fold in the egg white.

TO SERVE

Pour into small glasses and sprinkle with freshly grated nutmeg.

Index